Zhoozsh!

PROUDLY SPONSORED BY

Zhoozsh!

COOKING WITH **JEREMY & JACQUI MANSFIELD**

PHOTOGRAPHY BY RYNO • **STYLING BY JUSTINE DRAKE**

The authors and publishers wish to thank the following for the loan of props for photography: @ home, Banks, Boardmans, Woolworths.

Struik Lifestyle
(an imprint of Random House Struik (Pty) Ltd)
Company Reg. No. 1966/003153/07
80 McKenzie Street, Cape Town 8001
PO Box 1144, Cape Town, 8000, South Africa
www.randomstruik.co.za

First published in hardcover in 2007 by Struik Publishers
Reprinted in 2007, 2008 (twice)
This edition published in softcover in 2009

Copyright © in published edition: Random House Struik (Pty) Ltd 2007, 2009
Copyright © in text: Jeremy and Jacqui Mansfield 2007, 2009
Copyright © in photographs: Ryno/Images of Africa 2007, 2009

All rights reserved. No part of this publication may be reproduced, stored in a retrieval system or transmitted, in any form or by any means, electronic, mechanical, photocopying, recording or otherwise, without the prior written permission of the publishers and the copyright holders.

Publisher: Linda de Villiers
Managing Editor: Cecilia Barfield
Editor and Indexer: Joy Clack
Designer: Beverley Dodd
Photographer: Ryno
Cover Photographer: Mark Lanning
Stylist: Justine Drake
Cover Stylist: Ivan van der Boogaard
Proofreader: Tessa Kennedy

Reproduction: Hirt & Carter Cape (Pty) Ltd
Printing and binding: Kyodo Nation Printing Services Co., Ltd

ISBN 978-1-77007-785-0

Over 40 000 unique African images available to purchase from our image bank at www.imagesofafrica.co.za

Contents

Foreword by Billy Gallagher 6

Foreword by Terry Volkwyn 7

From the authors 8

In the beginning … 10

Mains 36

But wait, there's more! 106

Desserts 126

Pantry basics 140

Conversion charts 141

Index 142

Acknowledgements 144

When the phone rings at 5:30 in the morning and it's Mansfield, I just know it's going to be about something exciting and unusual. I was right. Jeremy told me that he and Jacqui were going to write a cookbook with a spin, with pizzazz and zhoozsh. What a great idea! I know Jeremy is creative and extremely capable in the kitchen. But I also know Jacqui's interest in food extends only to the dessert table and I'm not sure she knows where the kitchen is in their home.

The friendship between Jeremy and me goes back a long, long way. Even though we differ on the choice of football clubs we support, our love for food has seen us indulge in some great meals together. Reinforced by copious amounts of various beverages.

The more we spoke about the concept for the book (and I understood Jacqui's involvement would be on the anecdotal rather than the culinary side), the more excited I became and knew it would be a smash hit. Not only would it include nice, easy, practical and affordable recipes, all given the magical Mansfield touch, but their love of the bush and globetrotting adventures would provide the background for many of the dishes. This is what makes this not only a practical cookbook but a wonderful insight into Jeremy and Jacqui's lives.

Zhoozsh, I know what you are thinking: What an unusual name for a cookbook. I believe it is a great title and sums up the philosophy and character of what they have achieved. Take a lovely dish and make it even better by zhoozshing it up with a touch of magic. Food and cooking are meant to be fun. There is nothing better than getting into the kitchen and experimenting with a bunch of ingredients. It is the most relaxing therapy, and not only that, it helps you win friends and influence people! Everyone loves a generous cook and the old saying, 'never trust a skinny chef' is very apt here with regards to the larger-than-life Chef Mansfield.

Many people may not be aware that Jeremy was given the highest award for matters culinary when he received an honorary membership of the South African Chefs Association for his tremendous contribution in helping promote and gain funding for young, previously disadvantaged South African chefs to complete their apprenticeships. His commitment to the cooking fraternity is well known among the chefs and he enjoys great affection.

I have been an ardent collector of anything to do with culinary information, having spent the last 40 years involved and working with food, and I have quite a fair collection of culinary masterpieces that I have been able to build. I know this will be a wonderful addition. We all know that the shelves in bookshops are full of literally thousands of cookbooks, each one vying for the reader's attention. I believe that *Zhoozsh* is so unique, so easy to read and enjoy, it is certainly going to jump to the forefront.

I know you will love this wonderful book and I am very happy to have been asked to be involved by two wonderful people whom I regard as great friends.

Keep it cooking!!!

BILLY GALLAGHER   Southern Sun

Honorary President of South African Chefs Association
Honorary Life President of World Association
  of Chefs Societies
Director of Public Relations and Communications
  Southern Sun Hotels

When I first met Jeremy a decade ago I was actually quite fearful of him because he was so incredibly talented and displayed such a huge on-air persona. But it wasn't long before I got to know the real Jeremy – the Jeremy who is so completely passionate about life.

Behind his jovial character and endless beer praising, lies a soft and caring soul who's forever striving to find ways of helping improve the lives of those less fortunate; putting an end to animal cruelty; and rallying up support from his listeners to help join in his quest to really make a difference.

Among Jeremy's many passions lies his passion for food. One would be forgiven for thinking that the best dish Jeremy could whip up is a fried egg on toast or an overfilled cheese sandwich. The truth is, cooking is perhaps one of Jeremy's biggest talents – a hidden talent that up until now was reserved exclusively for the taste buds of family and friends.

Jeremy is an explorer of food who can take an ordinary meal and make it into something magnificent. His personality really shines in the dishes he makes. He is not a cuisine chef obsessed with perfection. You won't find him serving carrots carved in the shape of flowers nestled on top of a steak so tiny, one would mistake it for garnish. Instead his food mimics his true character – soulful, rich, warm, friendly and comforting.

Not only is this recipe book the perfect accompaniment for any food enthusiast, but it really gives people the chance to get a taste of 'the real' Jeremy, and what a deliciously, wonderful experience that is.

TERRY VOLKWYN
CEO Primedia Broadcasting

From the Authors

Maybe it was helping my mom, Veronica, the wielder of the wooden spoon for various reasons – one of which was purely for disciplinary purposes – bake mounds of biscuits before Christmas. Maybe it was our domestic worker Agnes Zenani's samp and beans gently bubbling on the stove when I got home from school for lunch. I don't know. But something triggered a love for cooking.

Since then two events have influenced my time in the kitchen. I was diagnosed with Crohn's disease and ulcerative colitis and was told to cut out red meat. And I met my wife Jacqui, a vegetarian. I had to change my menus and my lifestyle, which I did and am much happier for.

Some of these recipes are a reflection of that. Some are a reflection of the degenerate mates I surround myself with. Friends and food are my two cornerstones, coupled with the fact that when I am stressed I cook. I find it the most relaxing pastime. We travel a lot and I have picked up tips and recipes from our journeys and incorporated them into my cooking. *Zhoozsh* is a compilation of our life and lifestyle, combined with some of the places we have been to and what I have learned to apply in the kitchen… with, as the Beatles say (boy, am I giving my age away!!), a little help from my friends.

There are two things that have happened in my life that I will be eternally thankful for. The first is I have a home with a kitchen in which I can de-stress. The second is I have Jacqui. A wife who keeps the hell out of the kitchen.

My love, stay out of the kitchen, and I will always stay in your life.

Jeremy

Joburg Team: Peter Mabizela, James Khoza, Klaus Beckmann, Jeremy, Nick Msibi

Cape Town Team: Tiane Adams, Jeremy, Gouwah Kaffoor, Sivan Naidoo, Mark Goliath

I adore my sister Karin and I know she loves me. She is always concerned for my welfare and was convinced I would starve to death or die of malnutrition. She insisted a packet of Marie biscuits, half a packet of marshmallows, two gherkins and a cup of tea do not constitute supper.

She bought me my first and only cookery book – *Help! My Apartment Has A Kitchen*. I like the cover, the only part of the book I have read.

Fortunately the good Lord decided to send me not only someone who could cook but someone who loves cooking. Ours is a match made in the kitchen. When I met Jeremy I had food in the fridge older than he was. Between his expertise and creativity, and my lack of both interest and ability, we have come up with easy recipes that even I, with my cooking allergy (flares up horribly in the kitchen), will make.

If your Mr Delivery bill is higher than your grocery bill this book is for you. If you think making dinner means picking up the phone and making reservations, and if the only items you can swiftly locate in your supermarket are toilet paper, cigarettes, coffee, chocolates and bread, or if you can't cook this book is for you. Jeremy wrote the captions (my handwriting is illegible) and we both contributed anecdotes. Peas be with you.

PHOTOGRAPHER: NICK BOULTON

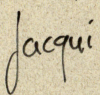

- **Conceptualised in** Maia, Seychelles.
- **Compiled in** the Rocky Mountains, Canada; Spurwing Island, Zimbabwe; Sabi Sabi and Simbambili, Sabi Sand Game Reserve, South Africa.
- **Developed in** the Sandton and Cape Sun kitchens, South Africa.

Take note: Everything in this book is based on a recipe for four, unless otherwise obvious, and is made with fresh ingredients, although I have no problem with replacing fresh with good bottled spices and neither should you. We need to do this when we are travelling in remote areas.

We don't mention adding salt and pepper in every recipe. Do what feels right for you!

In the

Beginning . . .

Creamy Caesar Salad

Globally, this is the tastiest version of this well-known salad I've ever had. It was the first time I'd seen it prepared with the dressing at the bottom of the salad bowl and not poured on top. Canada is a favourite destination of ours, eh? (That's how so many Canadians end their sentences, with a short eh? Kinda like our 'hey'.) I'm addicted to skidoo-ing (snowmobiling), bit of a snag that, what with living in SA and all. I first skidooed when we stayed at a snowbound lodge in the Rockies. Like many places out west, it was built by the railroad to encourage settlement and tourism. We loved this excerpt about Storm Mountain Lodge from a 1923 Canadian Pacific Railway promotional article: 'Awaiting you this year in the Canadian Pacific Rockies are a chain of eight Bungalow Camps forming one of the finest centers for unconventional, old-clothes vacations in the heart of this most magnificent mountain region.' Yeah, we are definitely hooked on old-clothes vacations!

Cook 4 rashers streaky bacon until crisp (see Macaroni Cheese, page 44). Allow bacon to cool. Make croutons.

Crush 3 tsp garlic, and then add 1 Tbsp freshly grated Parmesan cheese, 1 Tbsp lemon juice, 1 tsp mustard powder, 2 egg yolks (keep 1 egg white for later), and about 8 shakes of Worcestershire sauce. Mix well.

While mixing, gradually add 180 ml olive oil until you have a thick, smooth paste. Whisk the reserved egg white to soft peak stage and mix in. The dressing should now look like thin custard. Pour it into a large salad bowl.

Roughly chop in a cos lettuce. Toss with the crunched up bacon when ready to serve. Sprinkle with a bit more grated Parmesan cheese and add the croutons to zhoozsh it up.

How's this for a luggage transfer - Storm Mountain Lodge, Canadian Rockies

Dogsledding. Of course my face looks like that - I'm doing all the work

Ali's Oriental Beef Salad

Ali, a.k.a. Mrs Chifamba (because her husband drinks such vast quantities of Johnny Walker and the logo is of a man walking … chifamba is 'to walk' in Shona), is married to one of my best mates, Grant. Ali is responsible for 83% of Woolies' turnover in Joburg's northern suburbs. Quantities for any recipe of Ali's are always based on ingredients purchased at that store. Good thing her husband is no longer a Zimbabwean tobacco trader earning trillions of Zim Monopoly dollars, but a tobacco trader earning in a decent currency now. Ali regularly spends the equivalent of Zim's annual GDP at her local Woolies.

Take a 600 g beef fillet. Grind equal portions of black peppercorns and coriander seeds, enough to thoroughly coat the meat. Place the encrusted fillet on a baking tray and into a preheated 220 °C oven for about 35 minutes. The outside will look like charcoal, but the inside will still be rare.

Arrange the following greens on a platter: 250 g baby spinach leaves, 100 g green beans (first blanched in boiling water for about 30 seconds), 2 sliced radishes, 30 g shredded fresh coriander, and 30 g fresh mint leaves.

Prep the dressing by mixing together 2 Tbsp hoi sin sauce, 2 Tbsp white rice wine vinegar, 1 Tbsp sugar, 1 Tbsp soy or fish sauce, 1 tsp finely chopped chilli, 1 tsp crushed garlic, and 1 Tbsp vegetable oil. (This is our favourite dressing combination as it achieves the right balance of hot, sweet, sour and salt, but play around with the quantities to suit your taste. To give it some zesty zhoozsh, try adding 1 Tbsp lime or lemon juice.)

Once the fillet has cooled, slice it thinly. Lay slices on top of the salad leaves. Pour the dressing over the salad just before serving.

Jacqui's hint:
Crush a packet of 2-minute noodles, place them under the griller and toast them. Watch closely though, as this does not take long and they can burn easily. Sprinkle the noodles over the salad ingredients before you add the dressing.

Chifamba + Miss-chif (Grant + Ali) on Lake Kariba, 'Babwe 2006

Hot Three-Bean Salad

Speaking of hot ... A while back, Jacqui nearly got herself into hot water with me. She was working at the Johannesburg Zoo and wanted me to meet Snuffles, the black rhino. 'He's very friendly and loves having his cheeks rubbed,' she told me. Lying on my stomach, I leaned over and rubbed his cheeks, which were surprisingly soft and warm. 'Let him suck your hand, he loves the salt, but be careful 'cause he tugs.' Jumbo, the big male elephant, had the enclosure next to Snuffles and, man, did he dislike him. As I was lying there stroking Snuffles with one hand, the other firmly in his mouth almost up to my elbow, Jumbo threw a large clod of earth at Snuffles. Startled, Snuffles snapped his head away and leaped backwards, nearly dragging me into his enclosure! It was close, but I managed to pull my hand free just before I fell in. While Jacqui was giving thanks that she didn't have to issue a press release – Top Radio Show Host's Shocking Death *– my finger ballooned. When I eventually went to a doctor he confirmed it was fractured, but I was too chicken to get it re-broken. I am now one of the few people to have survived an encounter with a black rhino and still have the proof!*

Heat 1 Tbsp oil and add 2 tsp finely chopped chilli, 2 tsp finely chopped lemon grass, 2 tsp crushed ginger, 2 tsp crushed garlic, and 2 Tbsp chopped spring onion.

After about 2 minutes, add 3 x 410 g tins (drained) of your choice of the following, ensuring not all three are the same colour, just from a presentation point of view: chickpeas (in my mind this is a must), butter beans, borlotti beans, sugar or red kidney beans. Heat through.

Eat hot or allow to cool. While cooling though, be sure to turn the mixture a few times to mix the sauce into the beans.

Snuffles – he who nearly killed me + Jacqui – she who introduced me to he who nearly killed me (check the cellphone! She could have used it to beat him off if I had fallen in.)

Lentil-Feta Salad

I love this pulse. Lentils are so underrated and overlooked. Forever associated with hippies, pacifists, sandal-bedecked muesli eaters and monks, they are one of my favourite foods. I feel a better person for eating the same food that monks and other 'good' people eat. I think they are on the right path – one with flowers edging it. Love this parable: A monk had two large pots, each hung on the ends of a pole, which he carried across his neck. One pot had a crack in it, while the other pot was perfect. After the long walk from the stream to the house, the cracked pot arrived only half full. The perfect pot was proud of its accomplishments, perfect for which it was made. But the cracked pot was ashamed of its imperfection, and unhappy that it was able to accomplish only half of what it had been made to do. Feeling like it had failed, it spoke to the monk one day by the stream ... 'I am ashamed of myself, because this crack in my side causes water to leak out all the way back to your house.' The monk said to the pot, 'Did you notice that there were flowers only on your side of the path, but not on the other pot's side? That's because I have always known about your flaw, and I planted flower seeds on your side of the path. Every day while we walk back, you've watered them. Without you being just the way you are, there would not be beauty to look upon and ease the long walk.'

This is such a colourful salad. You HAVE to use robot peppers (1 each of red, green and yellow), seeded, cut into thick strips and then blanched quickly in boiling water. Rinse them and run them under cold water for about 30 seconds. Wrap tightly in clingfilm to stop them losing colour.

Heat 1 tsp oil on low and add 2 onions, peeled and quartered. Fry, turning them for a few minutes until the onion layers start to separate. Add 1 x 410 g tin lentils and heat through.

In the meantime, mix together 1 Tbsp lemon juice, 1 Tbsp white or red wine vinegar, 2 Tbsp olive oil, and freshly ground black pepper in a serving bowl.

Add the peppers to the hot lentils as you take them off the stove and stir them through, then pour the pot mixture into the serving bowl dressing.

Zhoozsh it all up by adding 1 Tbsp chopped fresh parsley, 2 Tbsp chopped fresh mint, and 100 g cubed feta cheese. Toss and serve.

Count the cows — Jacqui doesn't qualify!

Outside Monastery, Viet Nam

comparing tummies

Jungle's Salmon Salad

Jacqui doesn't like to eat anything that has a face. Tuna in a tin is fine, but nothing with eyes. She wasn't keen on sushi, having formed a negative opinion without even trying it. However, she's now a keen fan. The secret is to start with the simple, basic westernized stuff like a California Roll: perfect rice, a prawn, crabstick or salmon, a sliver of avocado and seaweed. Or a piece of A-grade salmon or a parboiled prawn striped underneath with wasabi and perched on a mouthful of rice and dipped in soy sauce. If your soon-to-be-new-convert doesn't like any of those, chances are they'll always avoid sushi. But if they do like them, you can then move onto more adventurous stuff like eel or blowfish! Jungle is a good mate of ours, and not only is his sushi and sashimi the best in Joburg but he's an entertainer, knows all his regulars by name and makes everyone feel welcome. He's also a whizz with his razor sharp knives and miraculously can create a cucumber fishing net with his Japanese version of a panga, all while appearing not to watch what he's doing and telling jokes!

Dissolve 2 tsp sugar and 1 tsp salt in 100 ml rice wine vinegar. Slice 150 g salmon into thin strips and marinate them in the rice wine vinegar mix for 5 minutes.

Remove the salmon and mix it with 2 tsp chilli powder, 2 Tbsp Japanese mayonnaise (available at Oriental food stores), 20 g crushed peanuts, and 1 Tbsp chopped spring onion.

A great way to serve this is on a bed of thinly sliced cucumber strips. Garnish with extra spring onion and cubed avocado. For the zhoozsh factor, add a dollop of caviar.

Harro breeez. You have one more saki. I insist Jeremy-san

Jungle + Mrs Jungle (Tanya) with one of the legendary sushi boats.

Summer Salad

Before I met Jeremy I was living in my brand spanking new apartment. I'd bought it off plan, and had been there for about three months. It was a lovely place with a gleaming kitchen. I knew it had a kitchen because I passed through it when I entered the front door. One evening on my way home from work, I bought a 'heat & eat' meal for supper. When I got home, I carefully followed the directions on the packaging as it was the first meal I'd prepared in my kitchen. I turned the knobs on the oven to 'preheat' it (see, I know my cooking terms). Next thing smoke was pouring out of the oven and I hadn't even put the meal in yet! I whipped open the oven door only to find I had set fire to the instruction and guarantee pamphlet. I stuck to salads for at least another three months. This summer salad is one of my favourites. It even has all the major food groups, or at least most of them, and doesn't involve the use of dangerous electrical equipment.

You'll need: 4 cooked beetroot, 1 peeled papino, 1 cup cubed feta cheese (or 2 rounds from those tubs), a generous handful of rocket, and 4 or 5 sprigs of fresh mint.

Roughly chop all the ingredients and toss together with 2 Tbsp olive oil.

Sprinkle with toasted pumpkin and sunflower seeds – amaaaaazingly good!

Total confusion – Jacqui in a foodstore

20 mins later and she thinks she's finished!

Cycling on the walls of Lucca, Florence in Italy

Remember the TV series "China Beach"? This is where it was set. The R+R centre for US troops near Da Nang Viet Nam...

...trying to explain to Jacqui that it's not cool to wee next to a coracle on the beach

Fothergill Island, Zim

Smoked Salmon Quick Bites

We have a very modern relationship. At home Jacqui is more likely to be on the roof clearing out the gutters and I'll be in the kitchen whipping up some marvellous creation. It works for us. I was in Dullstroom on a boys' weekend and the whole bunch of us were in a pub (yes I know, strange place to find me!) when a mate who lives in the town arrived. He had these great boots on and I asked him where he got them. What luck – his store sells them. He disappeared to get a half a dozen pairs 'cause by now all the guys wanted them. I called Jacqui to tell her she wouldn't believe it but I was buying shoes on my boys' weekend! 'Oh really, sweetheart, I've just got back from the hardware store. We needed a new drill bit, and I'm installing the safe.' What a team! Jacqui has never been a fan of smoked salmon, but here's a damn good quickie she came up with.

Peel and quarter an English cucumber lengthways. Cut it into lengths of 5–6 cm.

Peel off strips of smoked salmon from the packaging and lay them on a flat surface. Squeeze a lemon over them and administer the black peppercorn grinder with gusto! Leave to marinate for at least 15 minutes.

Wrap the cucumber in strips of marinated smoked salmon. Lay each one on a rocket leaf and here comes the final zhoozsh! Mix 1 tsp wasabi paste (Japanese horseradish, which you can buy in a convenient toothpaste-like tube) with 1 Tbsp mayonnaise (this is our mix, but the proportions are really up to you and depend on your taste) and add a dollop to each salmon bite.

As I pointed out earlier, she's damned good at a quickie!

MAURITIUS

Potato Soup

Jacqui's mom lives in Ireland, in a quaint, quiet part of the country crisscrossed with low mossy stone walls and dotted with fat sheep. We were over there and the three of us were out shopping. Bored with their mission to deplete every store of Cadbury's Chocolate Finger Biscuits, I headed home to my mom-in-law Pat's place. As I unlocked the door I heard the alarm. Dammit! I didn't know there was one. As I'm frantically running around trying to find the keypad, the doorbell goes. Through the glass I can see a policeman: helmet on his head, black kit and Day-Glo vest. Sweating buckets, I can see he looks big, must be the bulletproof vest and submachine gun holder across his chest. I open up and see the guy is a motorbike cop in full riot gear – talk about rapid and extreme response. Better than anything I've seen in SA! I'm just about to throw myself to the ground, shouting 'I'm unarmed! I'm unarmed! I sort of live here!' when he flips open his visor and I see it's Pat's neighbour, an ardent biker. 'Now how could you be tinking such nonsense? Shoot you? Don't be daft. And that's not the alarm, it's just ta message alert beeping on ta answering machine.' You can take the Joburger out of the country, but you can never take the country out of the Joburger!

Ireland is the land of the potato and, man, do they know how to cook them (and drink at the same time). To zhoozsh this one up ask your deli for a piece of spek (smoked pork back bacon) about 2 cm thick. You can use a 250 g packet of rindless streaky bacon instead, but the smoked pork gives a better flavour.

Dust the spek or bacon well with paprika then cut roughly into small strips. Heat 1 Tbsp oil and fry the pork until well done.

Cut 4 large potatoes into cubes and chop up 4 large leeks. Add to the meat in the saucepan. Just cover the ingredients with veg stock (page 30), or water with 2 tsp Ina Paarman's veg stock powder, or a cube of veg stock. Simmer on medium for 25–30 minutes until the potato is soft.

Blend with a hand blender until smooth. Serve hot, with a sprinkle of paprika on top and a hot, crusty Italian roll (the 7-minute pre-cooked ovenbake ones from Woolies are perfect).

Me, Jacqui, her mom – the old bat Pat! – sister Karin and her husband Steve

Jacqui's tip: To bulk this one up, add a tin of butterbeans and heat through.

Pho (Vietnamese noodle soup)

Vietnam is one of our favourite countries … the people, the food, the countryside and the culture. When I first went to Vietnam you needed a permit to leave Saigon (officially Ho Chi Minh City, but everyone except humourless bureaucrats still calls it Saigon). However, now the country has opened and embraced tourism and the mighty American dollar with chopsticks spread wide. On this trip we headed to the Mekong Delta. We ventured into areas where few white faces had been seen since the defeat of the French and the Americans. We found it rather droll that the Vietnamese refer to the latter as The American War, while the rest of the world knows it as the Vietnam War. It was morning rush hour, around 05h00 (the day starts early in summer while it is still relatively cool), and the locals were seated at a small eatery having breakfast. Jeremy wanted to try an authentic Vietnamese street breakfast so we stopped. Lots of rice, lime, slivers of fish and loads of fresh sprouts. But what made it memorable was the carefully made-up elderly lady who made a beeline for Jeremy, crooning over him and remarking what a 'beeeg American' he was. He called her his mama-san and the two of them twittered away like he was some GI and she would accompany him Stateside! She was tiny, and in the photo is standing next to a seated Jeremy. I'm sure she would have been thrilled to go home with him and make him happy, very happy, 'cause he's number one! There are endless variations of pho (Vietnamese Noodle Soup), a tasty clear broth with additions being a personal preference. In Vietnam, it is a popular ăn sáng (breakfast) dish, but if you can't trade in your Pronutro for pho, enjoy it later in the day.

You'll need 2 chicken carcasses (ask your butchery for them; they have leftovers from their chicken breasts and other cuts and they're fairly cheap).

Any vegetables will do for this stock. I usually keep offcuts of carrot, leek, onion, etc. and throw them in in equal proportions, but I suggest the following combination: 2 chopped onions, 2 tsp crushed garlic, 2 tsp crushed ginger, 1 tsp finely chopped chilli, 4 chopped carrots, 4 chopped leeks, and 2 cubed potatoes.

Sweat the onions, garlic, ginger and chilli together in a splash of oil. When the onion is translucent add the carrots, leeks and potatoes. Break up the chicken carcasses and add to the pot. Cover the ingredients with water and boil for 1½ hours, topping up with water as and when needed to ensure the ingredients are always just covered. Skim while cooking to remove fat. Strain.

You will now have about 1 litre of clear veg soup, which will probably need salt. Rather try 1 Tbsp fish sauce instead. This vile-smelling, but effective salt substitute can be bought at any Oriental and most mainstream supermarkets these days.

This soup can be used immediately or can be frozen for up to three weeks in an airtight container and reheated when needed. Before serving, heat thoroughly and throw in a cup of 2-minute noodles and cook them (duh!) for 2 minutes.

Tip: Make double the quantity. Use half for pho. Leave the other half in the pot and boil away until there's about a third left. Freeze this as a stock.

Jacqui's hint: You can set aside the remainder of the strained chicken and vegetable mixture for use in the Canine Cuisine recipe (page 124).

Your additions to this steaming mixture are endless, but my favourites are: 100 g chopped fresh coriander, 100 g bean sprouts, 50 g chopped spring onion, 1 tsp chopped chilli (if you want a bit of a bite), and 1 cup finely shredded pre-cooked chicken.

Simply place equal portions of these extras on top of each big serving bowl of hot soup.

surrounded by adoring fans!

and this one — who wants to marry me!

Vegetable Soup

One of the people I respect most in the world is Pamela Anderson. She has such great ... values. Not only is she an avid vegetarian, she is also an anti-fur lobbyist. I so admire her. I'm fortunate in that my work brings me in contact with some pretty well-known (and mostly likeable) celebrities: Madiba, the Clintons, Anastasia, Bono, Charlize Theron and Francois Pienaar. I haven't had the pleasure of meeting Pam yet, but I have got dopped with Wesley Snipes, taught Brian May the lyrics to Nkosi Sikelel' iAfrika, downed tequila oysters backstage with Glen Frey and chatted with Don Henley from The Eagles at their Twickenham concert, and spent time with Ronan Keating at his Kirstenbosch concert. But the frostiest celeb by far was Anna Kournikova. I met her at the airport where she was en route to Sabi Sabi's Earth Lodge. I knew she would be staying in the Amber Suite, the same place I always stay when I go there. Perhaps my opening statement might have had something to do with it: 'So, tonight you're sleeping in my bed.'

This recipe can be used as a base for any veg soup or, once made, can be reduced by half as a veg stock. It's a great way to use up veg offcuts that you have accumulated. It can be frozen for up to three months. I prefer to keep my base soup/stock VERY basic and then add stuff later.

In 1 Tbsp oil, fry up 2 chopped onions and 2 tsp crushed garlic. Then add your base root veggies, 4 carrots, leeks, turnips, parsnips and the like. (The only one I don't use here is potato, as it tends to overpower the other tastes and defeats the object of this soup/stock, which is to achieve a clear reduction.)

Stir-fry the veg for 5 minutes. Now add your leaf veggies, chopped celery and parsley, once again in equal proportions.

Cover with water (you may want to add 2 tsp Ina Paarman's veg stock powder to boost it) and boil for 40 minutes. It should, once strained, yield about 500 ml of clear soup, enough for 4 people. (Set the rest of the strained veggies aside to cook in your Canine Cuisine, page 124.)

Serve with hot bread; one of those oven-baked ciabattas is perfect.

Once you have this in the pot or freezer, the possibilities are endless. Use this as a veg soup on its own, as above; reduce by half to use as a stock; or enhance by adding 1 full head of cauliflower, broccoli or cabbage (or a combination of all three), chopped, and boil for 20 minutes. Blend together.

Jacqui's tip: If you really want to zhoozsh up this soup, make it a mock French onion soup. Take a slice of wholewheat bread. Smear with a butter and freshly ground garlic mix (to your taste). Cover with thinly sliced red onion sprinkled with grated Parmesan cheese and breadcrumbs. Grill. Float on top of the soup before serving.

Hot & Sour Fish Soup

I can always tell if Jeremy has had a bad day. Many people think he's home by 09h30, but it is usually around four in the afternoon, as he has meetings, presentations, recordings, prep for the next day's show and more. If he comes home and whips up a quick 15-minute meal I know it hasn't been too bad. But if he storms in saying, 'I need to cook!', and then spends the next few hours chopping, slicing, dicing and wok-ing (whatever) while listening to Johann Pachelbel's Kanon, and produces four or five meals, I know it's been a very tough, very long day. I am still astounded that anyone would choose to relax this way! Haven't people heard of bubble baths, back massages, chocolate, a riveting book, mindless TV sitcoms, target shooting or walking the dogs as effective stress busters?! As this recipe takes a little longer than 15 minutes, I'd say it was a good indicator that he had a difficult yet rewarding day. This recipe is a little more complicated than some of the others in that you may have to visit an Oriental supermarket to get some of the ingredients.

First you need to make the stock. Dissolve 2 tsp tamarind paste in 3 Tbsp water. Strain to remove seeds and skin. Take 1 litre water and, while bringing it to the boil, add the tamarind, 2 kaffir lime leaves, 4 tsp finely chopped chilli, and 2 tsp crushed ginger. Boil for 15–20 minutes then strain and discard the solids. Set aside.

In the same saucepan, heat 1 Tbsp oil and fry 1 medium chopped onion until soft.

Add the reserved stock and, while you are bringing it to the boil for the second time, chop up 1 x 230 g tin of water chestnuts and 200 g chopped bok choy or spinach. Add and simmer for 5 minutes, then crank up the heat and add 100 g fresh coriander and 400 g fish (hake is best here).

Boil for 5 minutes, and then add 1 Tbsp each of soy and fish sauce. Allow to boil once, and then serve immediately.

The Best Place to Be — at home in my kitchen.

Ginger Coco Chicken Soup

One of our best trips to Vietnam involved kayaking in Ha Long Bay. You head out in these beautiful wooden junks and, apart from sleeping and swimming, you do nothing but eat. Mealtimes are leisurely; with so many courses it's just as well you can get some exercise.

Bring 1 x 410 ml tin of coconut milk to the boil in a pot. Add 1 Tbsp crushed ginger, 1 Tbsp finely chopped lemon grass, 1 tsp brown sugar, 1 tsp finely chopped chilli, and boil for 5 minutes. Strain and discard what stays behind in the sieve.

In the same pot, simmer and stir continuously 100 g chopped oyster or straw mushrooms (available from Oriental food stores and certain supermarkets), 200 g cubed chicken breast, and 2 Tbsp each of fish sauce and lemon juice, until the chicken changes colour.

Add the strained sauce and simmer for about 5 minutes. Serve hot or cold, with a garnish of chopped fresh mint.

Ha Long Bay

Our Junk

Mains....

Jacqui's tip: For presentation, cut off the roots of some spring onion and then simply slice each one horizontally in half, root-end to green top-side.

Cheers from (another) roadside pub in the Far East

Noodle, Tofu & Smellee Wee Crunchee

Tofu. Tofu. Tofu. Especially when she hits 40. Guys, believe me, I know. I may have bullshitted you about a lot of things on air, but believe me on this one. It's true, I swear. You will thank me. Tofu is high in plant phytoestrogens and has been proven to ease menopausal symptoms. SO START COOKING WITH IT … OK … BEFORE SHE RIPS YOUR … tofu off … know what I mean? C'mon okes, no-one is macho enough to compete against menopause month after month after month. So put aside your meat mentality and show her your more gentle side. Your real reason for suddenly using tofu is on a need-to-know basis. And she doesn't need to know. Rather tell her the isoflavones in tofu are good for lowering bad cholesterol. And it's a wonder food that can even reduce the risk of breast cancer (SEE how much you love her!?) as well as prostate cancer. Moving along, but staying with all issues healthy, I've been told that asparagus is good for removing toxins from your system. Allegedly, that's why your urine smells so much stronger after eating it. Don't take my word for it … take a slash and find out for yourself!

Buy the tofu. 300 g. You get it in various forms. I always prefer firm, as does Jacqui (nudge, nudge). Cut it into bite-size cubes.

Mix together 3 Tbsp soy sauce, 1 Tbsp sesame oil, 2 tsp crushed ginger, and then lay the tofu in the sauce to marinate for 1 hour. Swish it around every 15 minutes or so to make sure it marinates evenly. Remove and drain on paper towel for 15 minutes.

Meanwhile, take a wok and boil up 250 g egg noodles in 1 litre of salted water for 3 minutes. Drain and rinse them under a cold tap and set aside. Heat another 250 ml water, blanch 250 g asparagus tips for about 3 minutes, then strain and set aside.

In the same wok, heat 1 tsp oil and fry the tofu pieces until brown. Remove with a slotted spoon and drain again on paper towel. In the same wok, flash-fry the asparagus tips and 125 g spring onions on high heat.

Toss the noodles back into the wok with the remainder of the marinade. Heat through. Turn out into a large serving dish and mix in the tofu pieces.

choosing dragon fruit

Couscous & Spicy Stir-fried Veg

Lots of people are wary of trying something a little more unusual, like couscous (no, it doesn't taste like chicken), preferring to stay with the more familiar noodles or rice. But step out of your culinary comfort zone and try this versatile base. People say any peculiar or unorthodox dish tastes like chicken; snake, human flesh, rare mushrooms, shark fin, whatever. But it's not true. We were having dinner on a pavement in Manila. A few stray cats had gathered around. The treats Jacqui always carries for animals were finished when this hungry cat comes over. So she leaned over and asked the guy at the next table if we could give his plate of bones and leftovers to the cat. We couldn't believe it when the cat gave a cautious sniff, wrinkled its nose, squinted its eyes and backed off. What was it, we asked the guy. Frogs legs, he answered. Aha! You see, not everything tastes like chicken!

Couscous, like all staple foods (rice, potato, mealie meal, etc.) on their own, is bland, so what you add to it is important. I prefer to go fairly fiery, but you can temper this to your taste. Also don't be scared to vary the vegetables you use for the stir-fry.

Cook 250 g of couscous as per package instructions and set aside.

In a wok, heat 1 Tbsp oil (sesame is a great choice here) and 1 tsp butter. Add and fry 2 tsp crushed ginger, 2 tsp finely chopped lemon grass, and 2 tsp finely chopped chilli. After about 2 minutes, add 1 Tbsp soy sauce and 1 Tbsp honey.

Cut into strips any or all of the following: red, green and yellow peppers, mini corn, spring onions, carrots, green beans, baby marrows. Flash-fry them in the wok over high heat, tossing continuously for about 2 minutes, depending on the amount of ingredients in the wok. They should all still be crisp and crunchy.

Place the couscous in a serving dish and make a well in the middle. Place the stir-fry in the centre. To zhoozsh it up, sprinkle with toasted sesame and pumpkin seeds, top with a dollop of sweet chilli sauce and garnish with chopped fresh coriander.

Jacqui's hint: There's nothing wrong with making couscous, and rice for that matter, way before the time and letting it cool. This is one of the ways Jem cuts down on pot and pan usage. In this dish he would make the couscous, set it aside and then use the same wok to stir-fry in. One wok, one meal – now that's real freedom! When you are ready to eat, simply spin the couscous (or as I mentioned earlier it's fine for rice too) in the microwave for 2 minutes, separating it with a fork every 30 seconds. It fluffs up the couscous or rice.

Jacqui's Girls — Nieces
Christy & Gina

Spaghetti à la Shani

My sister Shannon is the mother of my daughters (if you didn't get that, it just means I adore my nieces, who are the best in the world!). They are the most gorgeous, talented, intelligent kids on earth, destined for greatness. One will become the world's top fashion designer (after a wildly successful modelling career), usurping Tom Ford and creating an empire that will dwarf Dolce & Gabbana. The other will become an Olympian gymnast (without the eating disorder), first female astronaut to captain her own ship, discover a new planet, become president and eradicate global poverty. At the moment, however, they won't even eat their veggies. Shannon came up with this yummy recipe: full of flavour, taste and a dash of delicious trickery to make sure they get what they need to fulfil my dreams. I mean our dreams! I mean their dreams! Shannon tweaked their favourite dish, spaghetti bolognaise, to get the girls to eat veggies. It's now one of my favourite meals because you can increase the quantity of vegetables and lessen the amount of mince. The aubergine and onion become a type of minced meat of their own.

In a pot, fry 4 chopped onions in 1 Tbsp olive oil until translucent. Add 1 diced aubergine and 2 tsp crushed garlic, stirring until the onions are browned. Stir in 4 grated carrots. Remove the mixture and set aside.

In the same pot, heat 1 Tbsp olive oil and brown 500 g mince with 1 tsp salt (if you want to make this more of a veg and less of a meat meal, simply halve the meat and double the veg). Then add 2 Tbsp Worcestershire sauce, 50 ml tomato sauce and 50 g chopped fresh parsley.

Cook on low for about 20 minutes. Add more Worcestershire sauce if you want a richer colour. Add the carrot mixture, mix well, and heat through. Serve with spaghetti, cooked according to the package instructions.

Macaroni Cheese with Crispy Bacon

Speaking of things Italian and pasta … Montecasino sent us to Florence in Italy (yeah, I know, tough job, but someone's gotta do it) for a promotion. It was an unforgettable experience. Because of the time difference, we were up at 03h30. It was still dark as Sam, Harry and I hurried to the radio studio nearby, past the deserted piazza of the Duomo, the shuttered jewellery shops on Ponte Vecchio, sleeping pigeons, snoozing, riderless Vespas and the Uffizi art gallery, as the church bells chimed once in the silence. The studio was very rustic and informal: rough painted walls, large wooden shutters and with an inner courtyard. Harry was happy though 'cause they had a top of the range espresso maker and every morning he kick-started his heart with a shot or six. I'll never forget the sounds of the city as it woke up. Birds chirping, shutters rumbling open, scooters buzzing, shouts from flower vendors and the scent of coffee. Jacqui accompanied us once, but had a problem with her eyes. When I asked her what it was, she said: 'They're open.'

Take 1 x 250 g packet of rindless streaky bacon. This is the ONLY type to use. Fry on both sides in a pan until the fatty strips are translucent and it is easy to peel the strips apart. Lay them separately on a foil-lined baking tray and place them about 5 cm under the grill. **Watch closely** so they don't burn. As soon as they brown on the one side, remove the tray and drain off the excess fat. Turn the strips and repeat, draining and turning again if necessary. When they are well done, remove them from the oven and place on paper towel to absorb the last bit of fat. Cool.

The crispy bacon is great to have as a standby to crunch up and throw into salads, soups and sauces. You can make it, seal it and freeze it for up to 1 month, then just break off what you need, place it between two paper towels and spin it in the microwave for 2 minutes until hot. (This is the DEFINITIVE way to make crispy bacon. I am not a meat eater but I must say I do find it hard to resist a piece of bacon so crispy it can snap in two! So often when you order crispy bacon they bring you soggy bacon mutated into a burnt offering. Jem is the only person who knows how to do it the way I like it – in every way!)

Heat 250 g macaroni in 1 litre of salted water until parboiled (it should still be a little tacky when you bite it – *al dente*). Rinse under cold running water and drain thoroughly. Place in a deep baking dish.

You can make your own cheese sauce, but for speed and convenience you can buy a packet of ready-made cheese sauce. Add about half a packet of bacon that has been crisped to Jacqui's fussy standards and scrunched up into small pieces.

To give the sauce a bit of zhoozsh, add 100 g grated very mature Cheddar cheese, 3 Tbsp sweet chilli sauce and about 10 drops of Tabasco sauce.

Mix this into the macaroni and bake in a preheated oven at 180 °C for 20 minutes until heated through.

Jacqui's hint:

To finish it off and zhoozsh it up even more, mix equal quantities of dried breadcrumbs and grated Parmesan cheese – enough to cover the top of the macaroni – and sprinkle the mixture over the top of the dish once it is cooked. Place under the grill until it browns. Serve immediately. Once again I love this dish, as you can pre-do everything up to the baking stage and it keeps you out of the kitchen if you are having friends around. And with more and more people eating less meat, pasta is an acceptable main course.

On the walls of San Gimignano, Italy. (Check Jacqui's short short hair — I love it)

On the Icefields Parkway

On the frozen Lake Louise in front of the Chateau

Hard at work on this book in the Canadian Rockies — but never fear, a pint is near!

Lake Louise's Mock Lasagne

Only two mad South Africans would choose to drive the highway known as the most beautiful in the world in mid-winter. What the hell did we know? We wanted to see snow, and boy did we get our wish. The Icefields Parkway is 230 km of the most spectacular natural scenery as it snakes through the Rocky Mountains. But we saw squat because this massive storm front moved in and we battled blizzards, howling winds, near-zero visibility, iced roads and prayed we wouldn't get hit by an avalanche. The trip took over eight hours. Sometimes we couldn't even see the road let alone spectacular mountain scenery! They closed the road after pulling 32 vehicles from snow banks. We arrived at the five-star refuge of Chateau Lake Louise, where the parking valet couldn't believe we had done the drive in a standard car, without snow chains or even snow tyres. 'What the hell is a snow tyre?' we wanted to know. 'Oh, they're kinda like regular tyres but a lot more aggressive.' Sounds like they would do fine in Joburg.

Make 750 g (1.5 quantities) of Shani's bolognaise sauce (page 43) to use in this recipe or, if you're a big meat eater, try an extra 250 g portion of the Mansfield QC (page 75). With the sauce already made, this is a quick, sure-fire winner.

Boil 500 g fettuccine (yes, fettuccine! This dish involves no lasagne at all) in 1 litre of salted water. Drain, rinse and drain again in a colander.

Place half the pasta in a buttered baking dish. Pour over all the bolognaise or QC sauce and then top with the rest of the fettuccine.

Mix equal potions of Parmesan cheese (about 75 ml) and dried breadcrumbs and sprinkle on top. Bake at 180 °C for 25 minutes.

Summertime Pan-fried Kingklip

Johannesburg Zoo ran an event called Yebo Gogga. It was an entertaining insect expo to introduce visitors to and educate them about creepy-crawlies they might usually view only through a haze of Doom. One of the things I arranged was a Bug Braai. To lend it pizzazz and credibility we had one of the best cooks in the world, and the most decorated, Billy Gallagher. He cooked, battered (not that way!), stir-fried, dipped and generally zhoozshed up bugs like termites and grasshoppers to make them palatable for tasting. Jeremy's favourite was the chocolate-dipped mopani worms. There was a lot of global television coverage and Billy got calls from all over the world saying he'd been seen cooking bugs. To this day Billy says it got more reaction from his peers and friends than any other culinary accolade or event! Electing to omit the creepy-crawlies, Billy shared one of his favourite and easy to prepare recipes (I wouldn't know, but Jeremy says it is delightfully simple. Okay he didn't say 'delightful'. He said: 'F**k, that's simple!').

Season 4 pieces of kingklip fillet, about 160 g each, with salt, pepper and the juice of a lemon, and then lightly dust with flour on both sides. Seal in olive oil for about 4 minutes on each side. Remove from the pan and keep warm.

In the same pan, heat 50 g butter. Simmer 1 diced red and 1 green pepper for 5 minutes, and then add a small bunch of halved, seedless green grapes and a diced avocado. Heat through for a minute, and then add a squeeze of lemon juice and 20 g finely chopped fresh dill.

Plate the fish and pour the mixture over it. Serve with baby boiled potatoes and spinach.

Me & Bill — the most wonderful Man in the world, even though he supports Newcastle Utd!

Jacqui's hint: The longer you cook fish, the more water is released into the sauce. Keep it short. If you need to, remove the fish with a slotted spoon and set aside while thickening the sauce in the oven.

Jacqui with cornrows getting ready to do a Bo Derek "10" run on the beach.

Z! VILLA, ZANZIBAR

Zanzibar Fish Dish

I have a healthy respect for the sea. Generally I prefer terra firma – the more firmer the less terror. I also get ill. I loathe the patronizing remarks from those who don't suffer from seasickness. C'mon, it can't be that bad. Yes, it can, watch me while I throw up on your shoes. Jeremy is one of those yo-ho-ho and a bottle of beer types that can sail the Seven Seas or any storm and never feel under the weather. I've tried to describe how bad it is: You feel so ill you think you're dying, then it gets even worse and you wish you were. I'm also very wary of the large grey shapes that slide in the shadows. Ridiculous for a former game ranger, I know. Jeremy is fully aware of my fears so you can imagine his surprise when we were in a dhow off Tanzania and, from a pathetic seasick heap, I suddenly dived into the ocean! I'd spotted some dolphins and with a desire to mingle I raced after them. They were fast and I was not. I was left bobbing alone, the fathoms below me filled with all sorts of ravenous, ragged-tooth beasts just about to open their jaws and … I love my husband, the dhow came alongside and he plucked me up and plonked me down with a smile and not even a whatchadothatforareyouinsane. That night he cooked me supper, this delish fish dish.

Take 4 x 100–150 g fillets of a firm, white fish like hake.

Add the following to 1 x 410 g tin of chopped tomatoes: 2 Tbsp chutney, 2 Tbsp Worcestershire sauce, 2 Tbsp sweet chilli sauce, 1 tsp salt.

In a pan, heat 1 Tbsp oil and 1 tsp butter. Add 1 chopped onion, 2 tsp garam masala and 2 tsp turmeric, and fry until the onion is soft. Add the tomato mixture and heat through. Place the fish in an uncovered baking dish and spoon the heated sauce over it. Bake in a preheated 160 °C oven for 15 minutes.

Meanwhile cut green, red and yellow peppers into strips, cutting away all of the white inners. Serve the fish with a good dollop of the now thickened sauce on a portion of cooked Tastic's Brown Rice and Lentils. Garnish with the peppers.

Bar with a view — Island Style

Aftershock Salmon

I was fishing in a remote Alaskan stream for salmon and Jacqui was singing 'Teddy Bear's Picnic' (unusual), badly and off-key (usual), when a mama bear and three cubs emerged out of the undergrowth at the river's edge about 20 m away. Everyone froze, except the cubs, which continued bouncing about. Thank God Jacqui stopped singing. The bear was huge: large hunched shoulders and paws tipped with long claws that turned slightly inwards (amazing recollection of detail when you think you're about to die). She swayed her head, twitched her nose – they can scent better than they can see – and sensing that there was something out of place about the two objects in the river (us), she decided to leave with her cubs rather than engage in some serious disembowelling. She lumbered off with her still-bouncing cubs behind her. Just as well I was wearing kit this time as I often choose to fish kaalgat. Who knows how she would have reacted to my wobbly bits! Babbling with fear and excitement, we headed back to our cabin on the lake. I prepared this amazing aftershock dish from frozen fillets we'd brought with us when the floatplane dropped us off. Jacqui thinks my poor fishing skills were the reason we didn't come home with fresh fish, but I knew the bears needed the fresh salmon more than we did.

Switch your oven onto grill.

Boil 1 litre of water in a wok or deep frying pan. Add 250 g egg noodles, 1 tsp oil and 1 tsp salt. Cook noodles on high for 3 minutes, drain and then add 1 cup each of chopped coriander and parsley and 1 Tbsp chopped mint. Toss and set aside.

In the same wok, heat 1 Tbsp oil. Sear 4 pieces of salmon (about 200 g each, skin on) on the non-skin side for about 20 seconds. Place the salmon skin-side up in a baking dish. Use paper towel to dab the skin dry and then grind salt liberally over it.

Place the dish directly under the grill, ensuring the salmon is about 15 cm from the griller itself. When the skin starts to blister into big bubbles (about 4 minutes), remove from the oven and serve immediately on top of the noodles.

Some fishermen will do ANYTHING for a little nibble! Alaska '99

Our "home" in Alaska

Jacqui's tip: This is a great recipe for a small dinner party. Jeremy does everything up to the grilling stage a few hours before our friends arrive. When we are ready to eat, he grills the salmon and spins the noodles in the microwave for a minute to reheat them while I have the arduous task of setting the entire table.

Sam, with a beer-ya-tiful broken nose after a bar fight (okay, walking into a glass door) Harry, Madiba and myself at an outside broadcast from his house in Houghton

Grandma's Fish Pie

Sam and I had been working together for about a year when I hatched another brilliant and incredibly financially rewarding idea to make pots of money for the station. The team executed the concept flawlessly, the client paid up and the enormous commission cheque went into the pocket of ... the sales rep. Yup, that's right, we made nothing. Nada. Squat. Nix. Zero. Not even me, who had come up with the idea in the first place. We were rather peeved, so to soothe the blow the sales rep offered to take us out for lunch wherever we wanted to go. We wanted to go for sushi. The best and the most expensive. He agreed without argument. The idiot! He'd never seen us in action. The sushi was prepared in presentation boats the length of your arm. Sam and I ordered one. 'To share?' asked the rep. We smiled at him. 'Each,' I said. That day Sam and I, under the disbelieving eyes of that rep, ate over eight hundred rands worth of raw fish. It was disgusting. It was wonderful. The way we shovelled that tuna and salmon you could have painted us black and called us Flipper. We both love fish, a passion Sam has passed down to her son, Christopher, although his tastes are a little more pedestrian. They regularly make Grandma's fish pie together because Sam does the cooking bit while Christopher helps by cutting up the potatoes with round-nosed scissors. Sweet.

You'll need: 4 portions of white fish (I use 2 of hake, 2 of kingklip), 2 bay leaves, 1 tsp mixed herbs or 1 Tbsp fresh parsley, 500 ml milk, 6 potatoes, 60 g butter, 3 Tbsp flour, 1 cup peas, 1 cup whole kernel corn, a knob of butter, 100 ml cream, and 5 Tbsp grated Cheddar or any other cheese of your choice.

Add the bay leaves and mixed herbs or parsley to the milk and poach the fish in it, leaving the fish to simmer until the milk is at boiling point. Take it off the heat, removing the fish with a slotted spoon first. Don't discard the milk. When the fish is cool enough to handle, crumble it into your baking dish. Wash and peel the potatoes, cube them and then boil them until soft in a pan of water.

At the same time, make a béchamel sauce using the milk from the fish. Melt the 60 g butter in a saucepan over a very low heat. Add the flour, bit by bit, stirring all the time to prevent lumps. When all the flour has been absorbed, add the milk 1 Tbsp at a time, stirring constantly, until you've added about half a cup, then turn off the heat and add the rest of the milk, stirring until you have quite a thick sauce. Pour this sauce over the fish and add the peas and sweetcorn.

Mash the potatoes thoroughly, adding the knob of butter and then the cream to taste. Top the fish mixture with the potato and sprinkle the cheese over the top. Bake at 180 °C for 20 minutes.

Sey-unique Fish

I've had the privilege of eating red snapper in only two places; once was in Fernie, a tiny Canadian town famed for its mountain bike riding and skiing. Strangely, I found the time to partake in neither. I was busy sampling their beers (I recommend the British Columbian organic lager or the Kootanee) and cuisine. Canada has many restaurants that offer Pan-Asian cuisine. But it was still surprising to find Yama Goya, a dynamic sushi restaurant, in this one-moose town. The other place was in the Seychelles, close to the Port Launey Marine Reserve. At a brochure-shot location, under a few nodding palms and a large Bodanmyen nut tree, William tends to his fire, chargrilling the fish he has just caught. He holds down whatever seasonal work he can: caterer, informal guide, truck driver. Easy come, easy go, his life is as simple and straightforward as his cooking. I enjoyed his Creole accent sans the arrogance of the French! William told us about returning to one of the far-flung Seychelles islands for the first time in three years and seeing nothing. 'Dem fishin' de place out,' he said. I shop according to the Consumer Seafood List compiled by SASSI (Southern African Sustainable Seafood Initiative), WWF (World Wide Fund for Nature) and Nedbank's Green Trust, and only buy fish that are on their green list. Check it out at www.wwf.org.za/sassi and ONLY buy seafood that has the SASSI label. If you have a query about the status of a fish, just sms the type of fish, e.g. kingklip, to 079-499-8795 and you will receive an immediate response with information on the fish, e.g. threatened. (Marvellous hey!?)

William used red snapper, but as this is a SASSI orange classification – stocks are severely threatened – we use 4 x 100–150 g (skin on) mullet (haarder), panga or santer. Marinate them for 15 minutes in 100 ml soy sauce, 50 ml oil, 25 ml lime juice, and 4 tsp crushed garlic.

Braai the fish over hot coals and serve immediately with a squeeze of lemon or lime and black pepper to taste. Delish-fish.

Snorkelling, Seychelles

Jacqui doing her mermaid impersonation!

William's offering — Stunning — but as we point out rather use one of the SASSI green category fish.

52°C Chiloje Cliffs, Zim

INFINITY
Pamushana

Pamushana Bream

Pamushana is an oasis in Zimbabwe. It is a five-star cliff-side lodge perched above a lake with ultra luxurious, super-large suites, each with an infinity pool and a Swarovski telescope gracing the verandah. The Relais & Chateaux cuisine is probably the best in the country. It's also a stone's throw from Ghonarezhou (Place of the Elephants) National Park. We went from the pampered air-conditioned splendour of this exquisite lodge to camping in the scorching January heat of Ghonarezhou. We drove to the outlook on top of the majestic and humbling Chilojo Cliffs. The temperature gauge in our vehicle showed 52 °C. Damn, it was lung-scorching hot! When we checked into the park the staff were exceptional: friendly, efficient and glad of visitors. How the hell they stay motivated I don't know, but they continue their anti-poaching patrols, flag-raising ceremony at morning parade, and someone still sits in the empty reception area waiting for visitors. We pitched our tent beside the Runde River, just downstream from the large bridge that was wrecked in the February 2000 floods and still lay like a concrete carcass. That bridge used to unite the north and south sections of the park. We grilled the fresh bream we had brought with us from the lodge under a trillion stars. Running water, velvet darkness, pennant-winged nightjars, one small fire and us in Ghonarezhou's 5 000 km². We were the only visitors in it. Zimbabwe and Mozambique bream is quite possibly the best tasting fish ever. Any whole fish, though, qualifies for this recipe in four easy parts.

Take the whole fish, gutted and scaled, and lay it in enough tinfoil to cover and envelope it in a baking dish. Cut a lemon into thin slices and line each side of the cavity. Pack the cavity with equal amounts of sliced onion, green pepper and at least 5 cloves of garlic. Salt the upside well (about 2 tsp) and then close and seal the tinfoil.

If you are a Vaalie or can't get your hands on a whole fish (sorry for you!), use 400 g hake in a baking dish and place the same ingredients on top. Bake the whole fish – or the hake – in a preheated 180 °C oven for 25–35 minutes, or until done.

Meanwhile, in a wok, cook up 1 cup basmati rice as per package instructions, adding 1 tsp turmeric. Drain, rinse and drain again in a colander and empty into another baking dish. In the same wok, heat 1 tsp oil and brown 1 chopped onion, 1 tsp crushed garlic and 1 chopped green pepper. Empty into the baking dish with the rice.

Remove the fish from the oven. Throw away the stuffing and flake the flesh off the bone and gently toss into the rice mixture.

Seared Tuna with Creole Coconut Curry & Parsley Polenta

Driving around Mahé, we stopped at a beach restaurant, a perfect place, right on the sand and you could go barefoot while contemplating the basic menu. Hmmm ... what to have? When we travel we always try to eat local foodstuffs and not things like pizza or any global fast foods (shudder). A few Seybrews later and I was ready to order. Fish. Jacqui had eaten nothing but fish since we got here and wanted something else. She asked what the Kari Sousouri was. Bat curry. Pass, thank you. These are bright-eyed, intelligent mammals that flap around the skies of Mahé, particularly at dusk, and are about the size of a hadeda. Never in a million years would Jacqui eat that! We headed back to the sanctuary of Maia where Jacqui had this amazing, drool-inducing dish. Subtle flavours, and no mammals were harmed. The Seychelles, and Maia in particular, are heaven on earth. It's the best place in the world for deluding yourself that the beachside luxury villa is your own. Apart from the trappings of fabulous wealth – the colossal suite, i-pod, giant plasma screen, DSTV, DVD, fully integrated sound system (indoors and out), enormous day bed, private beach, a butler et al. – the villa has the best bath in the world. If it's raining, you are surrounded by water in four soul-restoring forms. You sit in your perfumed bath water under the thatch roof, which sits in the middle of the pool and overlooks the ocean. Bliss, and free of curried bats.

Take a polenta loaf (you can get these from Pick 'n Pay Foodhall) out of its packaging, place on a baking tray, pour over 1 Tbsp olive oil and sprinkle 90 g grated Parmesan cheese over it, and then bake in a 220 °C oven for 45 minutes.

Meanwhile, in a wok, heat 1 Tbsp each olive oil and butter and sear 4 x 150 g fillets of tuna loin on both sides. Transfer to a baking dish and bake in the same oven for about 8 minutes. Remove and set aside.

In the same wok, heat a splash of oil and fry together 1 diced tomato, 1 diced onion, 1 tsp fresh thyme, 1 tsp chopped fresh coriander, 1 tsp finely chopped chilli, 2 tsp turmeric, and 2 Tbsp curry powder for a few minutes. Then add 1 x 410 ml tin of coconut milk and reduce by half.

Slice the polenta and serve the tuna loin between 2 pieces, with the sauce drizzled over. A heavy hand of black pepper and some chopped coriander will also do the presentation trick.

The 4 waters of Maia — rain, bath, pool and sea. BLISS

The bat was in an open cage and could fly out at dusk.

Simple Salmon Fish Braai

Jacqui is useless at bargaining. On the beach in Zanzibar she met a couple of tatty-clothed kids with hand-made dhows. She asked if she could buy a toy dhow from them. They were happy to sell one to her for a dollar. Oh no, no, she says, that's too little, I'll give you two. No financial whizz is Jacqui! Nothing wrong with everyone walking away from a business transaction happy.

Everyone says braaiing fish is tricky. Here's the simple solution.

Take 750 g salmon, skin on, and cut into 4 pieces.

Marinate them, preferably overnight, but for at least 1 hour, in a mix of 1 tsp finely chopped chilli, 1 tsp sesame seeds, 2 tsp crushed garlic, 1 Tbsp sesame oil, 1 Tbsp fish sauce, 2 Tbsp honey, a pinch of salt and a good dose of ground black pepper, and a handful of chopped fresh coriander.

Grill over hot coals. Serve rare. Easy hey?

Looking for a bargain buy? Avoid the 2 chicks in hats here! (See story above) Jax on beach with my mate Boysies wife Kay and dhow sellers

Seafood Stir-fry

Internet holidays. We had a doozie! It was a last-minute booking as we couldn't get into Cambodia and decided on the Philippines. We chose Palawan, way off the tourist map. We could 'frolic with turtles, explore the underground river, experience local cuisine and relax at the spa'. Sounded ideal. Hmmmm. Even after the six-hour transfer in a crowded mini-bus the hotel looked unwelcoming. Government architecture at its soulless best. A bureaucratic hostel of some sort? Set in a coconut plantation it was a risky business dodging the falling cannonballs between reception and our room. The holiday turned out to be … interesting. No turtles, a narrow seaweed-crusted brown beach (not like our glorious SA beaches), the underground river was half a day away, lovely local cuisine but no one spoke English, so we ordered blind every night, and the spa hadn't been built yet. Hammock stretched between two palms and a bungalow over the water? Try a dormitory-style room with paper-thin walls and a family next door with ghetto blaster playing 'I'm a Barbie Girl' 24/7. Our radar should have beeped when we checked in at Manila's airport for our flight to Palawan and the steward said, 'Good luck'. However, we did get to a tiny turtle-breeding island and spent the night sleeping on the beach on our sarongs. It was a full moon and we could easily see the turtle tracks from the night before. The next morning we saw lots of baby turtles and brightly coloured fish in the surrounding sea. It was magical and the highlight of our trip. Just was rather far and damn expensive to have the holiday highlight sleeping rough on the beach!

I always try to keep the following seafood in the freezer, purely because they can all be used from frozen and you can whip up something like this in minutes: hake steaks, crabsticks, prawns (preferably cooked, peeled and deveined) and calamari rings.

Take 100–150 g of each of the above. Prep the calamari as per Jax's hint. Cut the hake steaks into 1 cm slivers (easy to do with a big knife when the fish is still frozen) and do the same to the crabsticks.

Bring 1 litre of water to the boil in a wok. Add 1 tsp oil and salt and boil up an appropriate portion of egg noodles, as per package instructions. Drain and set aside.

In the same wok, heat 1 Tbsp oil, then fry together 2 tsp finely chopped chilli, 2 tsp finely chopped lemon grass, 2 tsp crushed garlic, and 2 tsp crushed ginger on high heat.

After about a minute, add 2 Tbsp each of fish and soy sauce. Reduce by half then flash-fry the hake, turning continuously. Add the rest of the seafood and flash-fry until heated through. Add the noodles and 2 handfuls chopped fresh herbs of choice and turn to heat them through. Serve immediately.

DON'T OVERCOOK SEAFOOD!

Ps. THIS will stink!! Fishsauce always does.

Jacqui's hint: The easiest and best way to prep calamari is so simple. Place calamari in a colander. For every 100 g use 1 litre of boiling water. Pour the water over the calamari. Done. It is now ready to be flash-fried or eaten as is. No more rubbery rings!

Jacqui on turtle patrol at dusk. Palawan Philippines 2005

*Just tasting!
Oh! by the way the T-shirt town is in one of my favourite parts of the country. Prieska, Springbok, O'Kiep, the Northern Cape and Kgalagadi National Park*

Greek Salad Dressing Chicken

Kevin Crambe is the Executive Sous Chef Western Cuisine for Cathay Pacific Catering Services in Hong Kong. If you can't face another day cooking for your family, imagine Kevin's day. In January last year Kevin and his team prepared an incredible record-making 74 465 meals! Bear in mind these are complete meals comprising an appetizer, entrée and dessert. So, really, it's more like 223 395 individual dishes! Admittedly, his kitchen is bigger than yours – the size of nine football fields, it's considered the largest kitchen in the world. Oh, and of course he does have a liiiiiittle help!

Heat your oven to 180 °C. Pour 25 ml olive oil into a roasting pan and spread the oil all over the pan to grease it. Place 8–10 chicken pieces skin-side up in the pan, evenly spaced so they don't stick together. Sprinkle with 4 Tbsp flour so that each piece is covered, then pour another 25 ml olive oil over the top of the chicken.

Now zhoozsh it all up with 1 Tbsp Tabasco and 1 Tbsp lemon juice.

Roast in the oven for 20 minutes, then transfer everything into a casserole dish. Add 2 chopped carrots, 12 peeled and halved baby onions, and 1 stick of lemon grass, halved lengthways.

Over all of this pour a bottle of Greek salad dressing and bake in the oven for 20 minutes, stirring occasionally to coat the chicken evenly. Brown rice with this is a winner.

Chef Kev at a Chef's Table in the CPCS Kitchens. Note face mask! The cleanliness and hygiene levels are outstanding – as is the food. (Actually he wears a mask becos he is ugly!)

Chicken à la Antoontjie

They say the heart of the home is the kitchen and Anton's is no exception. Anton is one of those nauseatingly 're-hatif' types that can do anything from paint a tablecloth to cook a seven-course meal, decorate the table beautifully, provide perfect ambient music, keep his sense of humour, the cats off the table, and prevent the dogs jumping up to greet guests. We've been to his home north of Pretoria and remained contentedly in the welcoming kitchen all day. It has a huge, deep and wide fireplace for a real fire (no click and hiss of gas) with an ample place to bak brood or warm food in the embers. There are comfortable, deep, sofa-like chairs, gleaming copper goodies, pretty painted plates, jars of fascinating South African goodies that Anton and Rick collect on their travels, a warm wooden table (wragtig it must have come off an ox wagon) and a sprinkling of contented felines. Everything is within easy reach and it's a kitchen that really works – practical and pragtig. We love it.

Cook up 125 g couscous according to package instructions. Mix with 1 x 410 g tin of chickpeas.

Rub 1 tsp salt and 1 tsp pepper into 8 chicken portions of your choice (I would go with thighs). Place in a cooking/baking bag. (This is soooooooo Anton. If you can make it easy, do so. And I have to agree with him.)

Bliksem into the bag (his words!) 50 ml chutney, 50 ml mayo, 100 ml apricot juice, 1 cup dried apricots and peaches, 1 cup diced carrots (6–8 carrots, depending on size), 10–15 new potatoes (washed, with skins on), 1 cup chopped onion (3–4 onions), 1 tsp paprika, 1 tsp turmeric, and 2 Tbsp curry powder (mild or hot, depending on your taste).

Close the bag and bake at 180 °C for 80 minutes. Open the bag and pour the contents over the microwave-reheated couscous-chickpea mix and then garnish with a handful of chopped, fresh coriander. Easy, neh?

Kombuis à la Antoontjie – one of my favourite places to "kuier", eat and dop

Graça & Madiba

15 August 2004

Mr Jeremy Mansfield
Highveld Stereo
Primedia

Dear Jeremy,

Graça and I as well as our family and staff, send you our best wishes on the occasion of your birthday.

We hope the year ahead is filled with prosperity and good health.

Please convey our best wishes to Jacqui.

Yours sincerely

Mandela

N R Mandela

This is my favourite picture! The day Madiba saw a ring on Jacqui's finger – he asked her why it took me so long to propose!

Madiba's Chicken curry

A lot of international celebs visiting our country want to meet Madiba and I think he enjoys meeting the rock stars and gorgeous long-limbed models. Who wouldn't? But when a certain British ramp-walker renowned for her temper tantrums was made his honorary granddaughter?! Puhleeeze! After a little rant on the radio, Madiba's daughter Zenani contacted me to say she agreed with me. I'd be a much more useful grandchild. No one impersonates Madiba's voice better than I do; I could conduct telephone interviews with the media on his behalf, call up heads of state, raise funds and so on. I'm South African born and bred and I could fill in for him at a moment's notice (after 09h00 of course). Zenani made it happen and I went through the acceptance ceremony where I was invited to join the family and was made Madiba's honorary grandson. They served possibly the best umquombothi (traditional beer) I've ever had. It was my pleasure and honour to make this chicken curry for Madiba and share it with him at his Houghton home.

Mix 1 tsp salt into 2 Tbsp flour and 1 Tbsp turmeric and use this to coat 8 free-range chicken thighs. Seal these well in 1 Tbsp oil in a wok or pot that can be covered.

Once sealed, remove the chicken pieces and set aside. In the same oil, fry 1 large chopped onion, 1 tsp finely chopped chilli, 2 tsp cumin, 2 tsp crushed garlic, 2 tsp crushed ginger, and 2 tsp garam masala for a few minutes.

Add 1 x 410 g tin of chopped tomatoes and about 100 ml of chicken stock. Heat through, then replace the chicken. Make sure it's covered by the sauce, and simmer for 45 minutes with the lid on. Garnish with a handful of roughly chopped fresh coriander and serve with basmati rice.

T(ha)ime-Saving Curry Paste & Thai Curries

This is a quick and easy basic paste which takes only a few moments to prepare and can be frozen for months. I got the recipe from a Thai chef living and working in Hong Kong, one of my favourite cities which I visit every year. We land early morning and I head off immediately for breakfast at the Devil's Advocate, a gathering point for expats and my friends when I'm in town. Beer, so much more than a breakfast drink! DUI is not an issue when there are so many ways to get home. If they say there's a bus every seven minutes – there is! Otherwise there are taxis or the MTR or tram and they run aaallllllll night! Jacqui's take that I love Hong Kong because of the Cathay Pacific stewardesses is nonsense. Yes, Lotus Blossom (not her real name), one of the attentive and diligent stewardesses, did ask if I would like my nuts warmed. But that's just good service and attention to detail. Did I mention that Cathay's lounge at Chek Lap Kok (love the name of that airport! I always picture people with heads bent, scrambling around checking their nether regions) has one of the longest bars I have ever had the pleasure to lean on? Always a great place to bump into old friends.

Throw the following into a blender: 1 medium onion, 1 Tbsp crushed garlic, 1 Tbsp finely chopped lemon grass, 1 Tbsp crushed ginger, 1 Tbsp ground coriander, 2 tsp ground cumin, 1 tsp turmeric, 1 tsp ground black peppercorns, 1 tsp fish sauce, and ½ cup chopped fresh coriander.

Mix all the ingredients together in the blender, adding oil to make a thick paste. Freeze.

To make a red curry, heat 2–4 tsp chopped red chillies (depending on how hot you want the curry to be, 2 tsp should be medium, 4 tsp should be hot) in 1 Tbsp oil.

To make a green curry, do exactly the same, but use green chillies.

Thai Curries

Heat the chillies as above and then add 500 g meat (strips of beef or pork, no fat), chicken (cubed breast or whole deboned thigh, no skin), or fish (hake or any firm white fish, no skin, dusted with paprika).

Or 750 g veg. Use firm veggies, such as potato, leek, broccoli, green beans, etc.

Or do a combination of the above.

Stir-fry to seal the meat, chicken or fish. Remove from the wok and set aside. In the same pan, heat 1 cup coconut milk and 2 Tbsp of your curry paste. Simmer for 10 minutes, and then return the meat/chicken/fish/veg and simmer for 10 more minutes. Serve hot on rice.

A pint with Clem Souter at the Long Bar, Cathay Lounge, HK Airport! Check all the spaaaaaaaace for drinking!

Jacqui's hint: To zhoozsh this up, try adding 3 Tbsp crunchy peanut butter to the coconut milk when you add it to the curry paste.

Mansfield QC (Quick Curry)

My school career was always tough. When I was just 5-years-old (poor little soul) my mother made me walk to Stepping Stones Nursery School on my own. All right, it was only three houses away, and a very quiet street, but STILL…! I progressed to Oatlands Preparatory School in Grahamstown where I excelled, getting mainly As and Bs (see Exhibit A – my report card – overleaf). After astounding teachers, influencing headmasters and impressing friends I moved onto bigger things – Kingswood College. It was there that I was the recipient of one of the most priceless comments ever. My Afrikaans teacher, Mrs Price, wrote in my report card that I should 'learn to talk less'. Ha! How things have changed. Now I'm being paid **very** good money to talk. I talk a lot. I share personal stories about friends and family with my listeners. Something I was already skilled in back in 1974. Mr Butler, our house master, noted in the same report card that I 'waste the time of the class by announcing irrelevant family news'. Some things never change!

Heat 1 Tbsp oil, 1 tsp butter, 2 tsp curry powder, 1 tsp finely chopped chilli, and 1 tsp salt in a pan.

After about 2 minutes, brown 400 g lean mince by frying it in the mixture. Add 1 x 410 g tin each of chopped tomatoes (with juice) and lentils and cook, covered, for 20 minutes. To zhoozsh it up, add 500 g of shredded spinach to the mix after 10 minutes, re-cover and watch it go!

(For preparatory classes)

DEPARTMENT OF EDUCATION OF THE CAPE OF GOOD HOPE

NAME OF THE SCHOOL

Report on Progress of Jeremy Mansfield

for the period (1) 30·1·70 to 25·3·1970 to

(2) 8·4·70 to 19·6·1970

(3) 15·7·1970 to 25·9·1970

(4) 6·10·1970 to 11·12·1970

CLASS Sub Std A.

ME — MRS WALLACE — MY 1st TEACHER

Subject	Report 1	2	3	4		Report 1	2	3	4
First Language:					Arts and Crafts				
Oral Work	A	B	A	A	Scripture				
Recitation	B	A	A	A	Physical Culture/Eurhythmics				
Reading	A	A	A	A	Neatness		A	A	A
Spelling (sounds)	A	A	A	A	Written Work			A	A
Written Work			A	A	Days Absent	Perfect Attendance	Perfect Attendance	4	1
Language Work					Late	0	0	0	0
TOTAL	A	A	A	A	Saved In SB 993	50c	55c	R2·30	R1·65
Second Language:									
Oral Work			A	A					
Recitation			B	A					
Reading									
Spelling									
Written Work									
TOTAL									
Arithmetic	A	B	A	A					
Health Education									
Environment Study									
Writing	A	A	A	A					

GENERAL REMARKS

Report 1: Jeremy appears to enjoy every minute of school and he has done good work.

Class Teacher: M. A. Hickman
Principal: E. M. Baines
Date: 25·3·70

Report 2: Jeremy is doing good work and making general progress.

Class Teacher: M. A. Hickman
Principal: E. M. Baines
Date: 19·6·70

Report 3: Jeremy continues to do good work.

Class Teacher: M. A. Hickman
Principal: E. M. Baines
Date: 25·9·70

Report 4: Jeremy has worked well and has passed Sub Std A.

Class Teacher: M. A. Hickman
Principal: E. M. Baines
Date: 11·12·70

KINGSWOOD COLLEGE
GRAHAMSTOWN
JUNIOR SCHOOL

Report for the Term ending 10th APRIL 1974

NAME: JEREMY MANSFIELD   CLASS: 3

Average Age (1st Jan.) 10:3   No. in Class 23   Rank in Class 11

SUBJECTS	CLASS AV. %	% GAINED BY PUPIL	RANK	APPLICATION	REMARKS	Teacher's Initials
Religious Education						P.M.J.
Speech					Good. Jeremy works well.	O.W.
Writing/Neatness						
English: Language Composition Spelling Reading	75	83	7	2	Jeremy has worked well this term. He has a good vocabulary and a vivid style.	M.R
Afrikaans: Stel. Taal. Mondeling	64	61	13	3	Jeremy's work will improve when he learns to talk less and work more.	
Latin						
Mathematics: Arithmetic Algebra Geometry	62	45	18	3	I am disappointed in Jeremy's progress. He must work much harder.	M.R
Geography	68	76	9	3	This is a satisfactory result but Jeremy must aim even higher.	M.R
History	58	76	6	3	Jeremy wastes time with irrelevancies	M.R
Science	71	76	9	3	Takes a keen interest. Making good progress	H.
Music/Choir						
Art/Handwork					Jeremy is not working with sufficient concentration. He has ability.	J.H.
Physical Education					Fail	B.J.
Xhosa						

For APPLICATION 1 is the highest and 5 the lowest.

Tennis/~~Tennisette~~ Good progress. S.J.B.   Swimming

Cricket/~~Rugby~~ U/11 B – Wk/k – batsman. Kd.   Athletics ✓ B.J.

REMARKS:

Jeremy is mature and assertive for his age.

House Master

Jeremy needs to be sat on firmly in class. He always wastes the time of the class by announcing irrelevant family news! His content subject results are good but his Maths let him down.

Master in Charge, Junior School

Headmaster — B.Gardener

Days absent: 1

Next Term starts at 8 a.m. on THURSDAY, 16th MAY.
Boarders return by 5.30 p.m. the previous day.

Pork à la Pom

My frightfully British mate Watto, despite himself, is an uncomplicated bugger. Loads of golf, wine, golf, Johnny Walker Black Label, some golf, his understanding and uncomplaining competent wife Julie, more golf and the kids are all he needs to keep him happy. His cooking is just as undemanding and uncomplicated … Try this … dictated to me in his frightfully British accent while peering down his nose …

Thoroughly seal 2 medium pork fillets in 1 Tbsp oil. Place them on a large piece of tinfoil, big enough to fold over all the ingredients. Conservatively add a liberal smear (by that I think he means about 1 Tbsp in total) of English mustard to the top of each fillet.

In the same pan, sweat about 10 baby onions, an equal amount of whole button mushrooms and about 6 whole peeled cloves of fresh garlic in a dash of oil. Add these to a mix of mini corn, green beans, carrots, patty pans and baby marrows and place them in the tinfoil.

Add an inordinate amount of white wine (this one we really argued over as I know what 'an inordinate amount of white wine' means to him, but we agreed, much to his disgust, on 200 ml). Seal the tinfoil and bake in a preheated 180 °C oven for 20 minutes.

Serve the sliced pork with some of the wonderful jus and the steamed veggies on a bed of basmati rice accompanied, at his insistence, by 'an inordinate amount of wine'. He is emphatic that there is only one wine that should be quaffed with this superlative English meal: Hamilton Russell Pinot Noir.

Watto + I contemplate the complexities of life — over another dop.

Note the till!! Doubt anyone would stick their fingers in that!

Pork Belly

Mark Drysdale and I have been friends since Sub A, when we met as 6-year-olds about to start school. No-one has been friends with me for longer. At Grahamstown's Kingswood College we were both in Jacques House. We were mates right through to matric. And still are, more than 35 years later. At junior school, my other best friends were Steven Glasser and Andrew Curtis. Only Drysie and I remain of this young foursome. Andrew was killed in a plane crash in the eighties. I was then working on the Capital Radio news desk and reporting a light aircraft had crashed into a mountain in bad weather. It was only two hours later that they released the names of the passengers who were killed. Andrew was one of them. I was shattered. Steven passed away in Australia last year, so you can understand what an important mate Drysie is to me. We have a lot in common. We both love to cook and are pretty skilled in the kitchen. His pork belly (which he insists isn't fattening and is low in cholesterol … yeah riiiiight!) is one of the best, with his kick-ass simple ingredients that elevate it from ordinary to spectacular.

Ask your deli butcher for a 1 kg piece of belly that has an even thickness of fat. Place in a baking dish, skin-side up, and get to work on the skin with your ground rock salt. You'll need about 4 tsp ground on the top.

Bake for 70 minutes in a 180 °C oven. Then remove and put the oven onto grill. Sprinkle some water on the skin and place about 5 cm under the grill. Allow to crackle and blister. Carve up and serve with roast potatoes (page 85).

Kingswood College Grahamstown 1980. Steve Glasser, Mike King, Andrew Curtis and Me.

Drysie + I doing what we do best — dopping!

Sweet & Sour Pork

Hanoi has one of the best Old Quarters in the world. You can see Cua O Quan Choung, the Old East Gate, an ancient remnant of the wall that once surrounded the city, sitting like an elderly and forgotten relative among the bustle and vibe of modern life. The streets are all named after the products the artisans and hawkers supply and make, like Hang Bac for silversmiths and Hang Ca for fish. There are lots of pavement eateries where people fold themselves up into child-sized plastic or wooden chairs (okay, maybe if you're Vietnamese there's not much folding, but for me there is). It is also the only city we know that has its own Border Guards Museum. Whoo-hoo. Despite official opening hours it is often closed. How ironic. My favourite place is Fanny's Ice Cream on the southeastern corner of Hoan Kiem Lake. Where else on the planet can you stand on a pavement licking com-flavoured ice cream? (Com is an extract from young sticky rice – don't know what you were thinking.)

Roughly chop up 1 onion and 1 green pepper. Add 2 tsp crushed garlic. Fry together in 1 Tbsp oil for a minute. Add 250 g lean pork, cut into strips, and brown well.

Mix ½ cup water with 2 Tbsp fish sauce, 2 Tbsp white vinegar, and 1 Tbsp brown sugar. Add to this 1 Tbsp cornflour (Maizena) and mix until the flour has dissolved. Add this along with 1 x 410 g tin (drained) of chopped pineapple pieces to the pork and cook over medium heat until the sauce has thickened. If you like, add some chopped fresh mint or coriander.

Serve with basmati rice.

HA NOI

Jacqui's hint: Add a bit of turmeric to the rice if you're serving it with the pork, as well as a handful of chopped fresh basil leaves.

Me and Mimi – Dimitri Macris – discuss food at his "Head Office" News Café, Livonia.

Jacqui's tip: When you turn the lamb while re-heating (after about 15 minutes), squeeze a lemon over the potatoes.

Leg of Lamb à la Grecque

The dogs love it when Jeremy cooks this meal. He always makes so much there are always leftovers, which the dogs enjoy with their dinner. And there's the bone for the dog that didn't get caught sleeping on the furniture. That's usually Alex, 'cause he's pretty smart. Although Jesse is the boss and leader of the four-footed members of the family, Alex is the wisest and brightest. He also loathes smoking and will move away, sneezing volubly, if someone lights up near him. Richard was petsitting. He told us that he was leaning against a ledge, talking on his cell phone. He placed a cigarette in his mouth while searching his pockets for a light. Alex jumped up on the ledge, leaned over, gently removed the cigarette from Richard's mouth and dropped it on the floor. Unbelievable! He was so dumbfounded he had to end his call. Jeremy tried it and sure enough Alex did the same thing again – gently removing the unlit cigarette with an apologetic look that said 'you really shouldn't, y'know'.

Take a 4 kg leg of lamb, bone in, and use a skewer to make about 10 incisions on one side. Crush 10 cloves of garlic and mix them with 4 tsp chopped fresh origanum. Use this to stuff the holes.

Mix 1 cup flour with 2 tsp each of salt, pepper and fresh origanum and turn the lamb in this coating. Heat olive oil in a baking dish, on the stove, and seal the entire leg.

In a blender, mix the juice of 3 lemons (soak lemons in boiling water for 5 minutes – you'll double their juice yield when you squeeze them), 6 Tbsp olive oil, 1 tsp salt, and 100 g fresh origanum, until thick.

Pour over the lamb and cover with tinfoil. Place in a 100 °C oven for 12 hours. Turn once to re-cover with the sauce. The zhoozsh part of this is once it is cooked it can stand for hours. Just turn it in its sauce. When ready to serve, remove tinfoil and bake at 200 °C for 30 minutes, turning once.

Serve it with roast potatoes: Peel and quarter 4 potatoes, then parboil them in a deep pan for 5 minutes with a bit of salt in the water. Drain the potatoes, turf the water out of the pan and heat 2 Tbsp oil and 2 tsp butter in it. Seal the quartered potatoes on each side in the oil and transfer them to a baking dish. Seal them again by sprinkling salt on all sides. Bake in a 200 °C oven for 20 minutes, or until crisp on the outside. This can be done at the same time as re-heating the lamb, in the same oven, at the same temperature. Zhoozsh, or what?

Use the leftovers to make lamb pasta (page 86).

Lamb Pasta

The BBFC (Big Boys Flying Club) often convenes at Giovanni Pane Vino for Roberto's fall-off-the-bone lamb. It's a chance for mates to get together and catch up on airline gossip and info. At one such BBFC meeting my good mate Don Hunter, a.k.a. The Big White Hunter, recounted an hilarious incident: A tired koffie moffie was fed up with an impatient and demanding female passenger. He was walking back to the galley, arms stacked high with snack boxes up to his chin, and as he passed this woman she insisted he clear her tray. 'Madam,' he snapped, 'I have testicles not tentacles!'

This is a great way to use leftovers from the leg of lamb recipe (page 85). Thinly slice about 100 g of lamb per person off the bone and set aside.

Heat 100 ml water in a heavy-based pan with 1 Tbsp each of brown onion and oxtail soup powder. Once boiling, add 100 g each of thinly stripped baby marrows and carrots and 100 g roughly chopped mushrooms (I prefer porcini, which give the dish a strong earthy taste, but button mushrooms are fine). Add the lamb and heat through, uncovered, over medium heat for about 7 minutes. Serve out of the pan with fettuccine or linguini.

Hard at work —

Actually I have just realised how few pictures I have of myself or with me and mates where this (DOP) is not present. I wonder who always sneaks them into the photos?

Jacqui's hint: This dish is even better made hours before then left to stand so that all the pulses absorb the flavours. Simply reheat then serve. Perfect if you don't want to be cooking when you have friends around! Great served with wild or brown rice, even better with pap, but then ensure you have a good amount of sauce.

Shin, Tomato & Beans

This terrific one pot meal (okay be pedantic – two pots if you include the rice) is great for a games evening. We enjoy entertaining at home and often have friends for 30 Seconds, Pictionary or Cranium. It ALWAYS involves much drinking. We state unequivocally that we are not responsible for any divorces resulting from 'You idiot! Of course it's a lawnmower!', 'How do you expect me to get it from that?!', 'He wasn't a cricketer! He was a founder of the ANC', 'Oasis is a band, not a desert watering hole', and suchlike. We've heard such gems as – 'Capital of Germany? Stuttgart. No! Not that one! The other one!' And who could forget 'Jesus' friends! Jesus' friends!' (The Twelve Disciples). But the absolute classic is still this: During 30 Seconds, and amid not that much alcohol, a card came up that had a certain nameless person huffing out short sharp breaths. No matter what we shouted, nothing was said. She just continued to hunker over, making these weird wheezing noises. Time's up and we ask her what on earth she was doing. 'How can you not get it? It's Lamaze! I was breathing like they do in the maternity classes! Haven't you heard of Lamaze classes?!' The card said Le Mans. It's a racetrack in France.

Take 750 g shin (the bigger the marrow bone the better) and thoroughly coat in a mixture of 5 parts flour to 1 of paprika. Seal the coated shin a few pieces at a time in a wok with about 50 ml of oil until browned. Set aside in a baking dish, preferably in one layer although it is not a train smash if you have to double layer it.

In the oil remaining in the pan, stir-fry 2 large chopped onions and 4 large sliced leeks. You can get creative here and add 2 tsp ground coriander or crushed coriander seeds and 2 tsp cumin.

Add to this and heat a mixture of 2 x 410 g tins of chopped tomatoes, 2 tsp Ina Paarman's vegetable stock powder (or 200 ml of your own, page 30) or a stock cube, and 2 tsp chopped fresh origanum.

Pour this mixture over the meat. Top up with boiling water if necessary to ensure ingredients are just covered.

Cook, uncovered, in a 220 °C oven for 1½ hours. Remove from the oven and add 1 x 410 g tin each (drained, but reserve some of the brine) of lentils, butter beans and chickpeas. Mix in the beans, ensuring the meat is still covered. If the sauce is not covering the meat, use a bit of the brine from the tins of beans to top it up. Return to the oven for another hour, stirring once after 30 minutes, and again ensuring the other ingredients are covering the meat.

By this time the meat should all be off the bone. If not, cook for another 15 minutes (this all depends on the thickness of the cut of shin).

Samp & Beans

Never send a woman to do a man's job. I asked Jacqui to buy samp and beans. She called me from the aisle to tell me she could only find samp and bones, and she wasn't going to buy that! Bone is Afrikaans for beans. True story, I kid you not! One of my earliest culinary memories of growing up in the Eastern Cape was of our domestic worker, Agnes Zenani, cooking samp and beans. Agnes used a battered old pot and the fragrances and tastes that came out of it were always out of this world. I was never allowed to help and it was a daily ritual watching her stir the samp while I sat on the ledge next to the stove with the dogs at my feet. Our kitchen was the central hub of my home life. There was always something being prepared. We ate at a huge wooden table and the large wooden toy box was one of the benches we sat on. I remember in wintertime if I wasn't keeping warm in the kitchen I was warming my feet outdoors by jumping in the fresh, warm cow pats. Little did I know that being in the shit would become a hugely successful career! There are two versions here, a vegetarian and a meat version. Both are gyppo versions of the traditional way of cooking this meal – quicker and easier and, at the risk of upsetting the Xhosa nation and the spirit of my Xhosa mother, Agnes, just as good.

Samp is always quicker to cook if it's been soaked for at least 4 hours, or even overnight, then drained. For the veg version, leave out the next step.

Meat version: Take about a 250 g cut of a good, bone-in stewing meat like chuck or brisket. Dust with paprika on both sides. Heat 1 Tbsp oil in a pot and seal the meat well on both sides.

Put the presoaked samp in the pot on high, with enough salted boiling water to cover the samp. Add 2 tsp butter and simmer on high for 2 hours, uncovered. Check that the water always just covers the samp when boiling, topping up when necessary. Samp should be soft, never mushy, when ready. Play it by beer!

When the samp is ready, add 1 x 410 g tin of drained sugar or red kidney beans, mix in well with 1 Tbsp butter and allow to heat through thoroughly. Keep uncovered and do not add any more water, but keep stirring occasionally.

'AGNES' NONTOZANELE ZENANI
16.12.52 — 14.9.91

Still loved. Still missed.

Jacqui's hint: Another dish best cooked hours ahead of time and then set aside to let the sauces mingle. When you set it aside though, give it a bit of zhoozsh by adding 2 Tbsp of chutney and mixing it in well.

A picture of innocence!

Sidney Nyoni + Me

empties after a morning fishing expedition

"Ndarama" - outrunning a typical Kariba storm

Jacqui + Guests on Game Drive

Sadza & Nyama

This recipe is courtesy of Sydney Nyoni, supplier of dop to Jeremy and mates and chef-in-chief of the Lake Kariba houseboat Ndarama. The lake is a regular water/bush breakaway. I love to get back to the bush where I was a game ranger. I remember once I had a group of journalists on a drive. The reserve was brand new and there was very little game and what there was was exceedingly skittish as it had been a hunting area before. If I saw anything interesting I stopped: a scrub hare, a tree that can assist your sex life (Buffalo thorn Ziziphus mucronata guys, if you must know), anything. When we stopped at a particularly large bark spider suspended across the road, I began the whole spiel about how they pack up their webs at night and so on. One woman got very close, her nose inches away as she examined the spider. She asked why it was called a bark spider. I told her it was because when they were agitated they made a high-pitched yapping sound similar to that of a Maltese poodle. She leapt back and I didn't have the heart to tell her I just made that up. I mean, really … who ever heard of spiders vocalizing? So, if that journo from Natal reads this: I apologise. It's not true. It's because when they sit on bark with their legs pulled in tight they look like a nub of … well … bark. Promise that's the truth. This recipe is different in that the meat (in African cuisine) is first boiled and then fried, as opposed to (the European style of cuisine) being fried, to seal it, then boiled.

Take 250 g stewing steak or other on-the-bone stewing meat. Cover with water in a pot. Boil. Keep topping up and boiling until the meat is tender and falling off the bone and all the water has boiled away.

Add 1 Tbsp oil to the meat and brown. Add 2 chopped onions and 2 chopped tomatoes and fry before adding a full head of chopped spinach. Add about 1 cup water for sauce. If this is too much, don't worry, just reduce and, as they say in 'Babwe, just enjoy.

Serve with sadza (pap). And eating it with your fingers is a compulsory prerequisite!

Oxtail

For a quickie, I leave home but don't go far – time being of the essence – just up the drag to the Morningside Country Club, or God's Waiting Room as we all call it. The average age of its members is about 97. It's convenient, quiet, and one of the few drinking holes that doesn't overlook a parking lot or road. Instead we can watch the old fogies bowl on the greens, tap a ball over the tennis net or we can bet on which Zimmer frame driver will reach the bar counter first. This is where I meet my mates at short notice for a dop and to discuss important things. Like what? Beer, women, the state of the nation, holidays and good food. My mate Spike (Brian Spilkin), whom I hardly ever see without the light of a fridge shining in his face, gave me this recipe one chilled Friday afternoon when we both needed/wanted to be out of home. If you have a slow cooker, this one is an absolute winner.

Heat 2 Tbsp oil in a wok until hot, then throw in 4 chopped onions. Add 1 oxtail and brown on all sides. Add 1 tsp each of salt and pepper, some paprika, and 125 ml each of Coke and red wine.

Simmer together for 5 minutes, then add 2 cubes beef stock, a packet of brown onion soup powder and 1 litre of water. Simmer for another 5 minutes, and then transfer to your slow cooker.

Cook for 12 hours in a slow cooker or 8 hours in a pressure cooker. The meat should be falling off the bone.

Another one to cook WAAAAAAAAAAAAY before the time. Let it stand, cool and then reheat on low for 2 hours before serving with mashed potatoes.

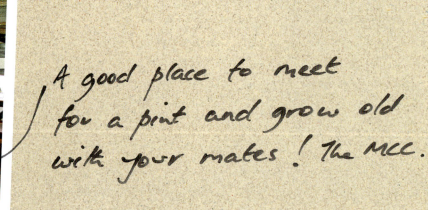

A good place to meet for a pint and grow old with your mates! The MCC.

Steak Casserole

In Joburg I'm up damn early, before 05h00, every morning to be on air, so on holiday I like to sleep late. We were on safari in Botswana in October, also known as Suicide Month. Everything is waiting for the rains. We were there hoping to see the endangered and elusive wild dog, so we jokingly told the ranger not to wake us for anything other than wild dog. Sure enough, the next morning, before dawn, there's a knock on the door and we're told there are wild dogs near our Duma Tau camp. We were up, dressed and on the Landie in less than five minutes. We found the dogs running and playing in the cool shadows of the reed beds as the sun rose. They passed directly in front of our tent – we could have stayed in bed and watched them play at the water's edge! Incredible, amazing and wonderful Africa. We were still talking about it that night when we ate this casserole, listening to hyenas' laughter under a sky solid with stars.

Boil 300 ml water and dissolve a beef stock cube in it.

Cut 3 green peppers into strips.

Coat 1 kg chuck or stewing steak in 2 Tbsp flour seasoned with 2 tsp paprika and seal the meat in a pan in 1 Tbsp oil. Place in a baking dish (with a lid) and sprinkle with 1 tsp dried thyme.

In the same pan, heat another 1 Tbsp oil and fry 2 tsp crushed garlic and 4 chopped onions until they turn brown. Add 1 Tbsp flour and then slowly mix in the beef stock until it becomes a smooth sauce. Add 1 tsp ground black pepper, and then pour this sauce over the steak. Spread the green peppers over the casserole. Cover and bake in a 160 °C oven for about 3 hours.

Beef 'n Hansa

This is the SA equivalent of the Irish Beef 'n Guinness. I might have tasted the latter in Ireland, but I can't remember. Jacqui's cousins took me on a pub crawl and they are the only people I know who can drink faster than I can. We drank to the Springboks, rugby in general, the cessation of 'The Troubles' and apartheid, Danny Boy and much more. I called Jacqui to tell her we were going to another pub – the sixth one I think – and we hadn't even gone 100 m! It was marvellous. We stepped outdoors into rain blowing horizontally and only took two steps before ducking into another traditional Irish pub. Ahh! I knew there was a reason I loved me wife – her Irish culture!

You will need at least 8 bottles of the brew to make this dish. The Irish will scream and shout, but this is better than theirs. Before beginning, open a Hansa and drink it.

Now take 1 kg of steak (the Irish use anything available, I prefer sirloin), cut it into cubes, and coat it in flour with 1 tsp salt and 1 tsp nutmeg mixed into it. Seal the meat in a pot in 2 Tbsp oil until thoroughly browned. (Have another Hansa while doing this.)

Remove the meat. (Be Irish, save water and put the meat into the lid of the pot. Have a Hansa.) Heat 1 Tbsp oil and 1 tsp butter in the same pot. Add 3 chopped onions and 2 tsp crushed garlic and brown. Add 1 tsp brown sugar and allow it to caramelize. Throw the meat back in and add 2 bottles of Hansa to the mix. (Open the sixth one and drink it yourself.)

Here comes the zhoozsh. Squeeze an orange and add a bay leaf to the pot before bubbling it on low, uncovered, for 1½ hours, or until the meat is tender. Add more Hansa if it gets too thick, but don't forget to drink some as well. (Another bottle is suggested, but more is better. Remember, the more you drink the better it tastes!)

Just tasting, that's all

I love all the preparation that goes into dish!

Girl with a gun. BEWARE! Actually, to this day, Jax is a hot-shot. She still drags me off to the range for a bit of de-stressing shooting. A member of the National Squad is still trying to convince her to take up shooting seriously.

PHINDA '90

Another Jem, sorry gem, from Jax: To reduce balsamic vinegar, which is great over any salad, pour an inch into a microwaveable cup. Bung it into the microwave and reduce it by half. It stinks – a really acrid throat-constricting smell – but the taste is worth it!

Ostrich & Polenta

Working as a game ranger on private reserves for many years, you do take flak for being female. 'Girlie, do you know how to use that thing?' referring to the .375 rifle we carried. Allow me to shoot the ridiculous hat off your head to show you, was not the reply I gave. Being prejudged because I was a woman meant I strove to be the best shot, best driver, most knowledgeable ranger there was. But still, sometimes I just got it wrong. Driving through a thicket of ilala palms I heard a deep, low booming sound. 'What was that?' my guests wanted to know. As I confidently stated that it was a wildebeest, probably making a challenge call to other males, an ostrich strode out. I lost all credibility. Even a first-time visitor to Africa knew the difference between the two. Boy, did I feel like an idiot. See, sometimes women aren't always right! This is Jeremy's favourite ostrich recipe.

Another easy option. You can buy a polenta (the Italian version of pap) loaf at most supermarkets. Brush it with some olive oil and pop it in a 200 °C oven for about 30 minutes to heat through.

Jacqui's tip: Zhoozsh this one up by making what I call a polenta sandwich bake. Cut the polenta loaf in half horizontally. Liberally spread sweet chilli sauce and sprinkle grated mature Cheddar cheese on one side before closing the polenta back up and popping it in the oven.

I usually get ostrich steaks at Woolies as the portions are perfect. Coat them liberally with ground black pepper – puhlenty of it! Grill over hot coals for about 2 minutes a side. They will be rare, the way I prefer them, but feel free to braai them for longer if you like, bearing in mind that there is nothing worse than a steak well done! Serve with slices of polenta loaf.

A good salad to go with this is a simple mix of baby salad leaves with sliced radishes, some olive oil and reduced balsamic vinegar as a dressing.

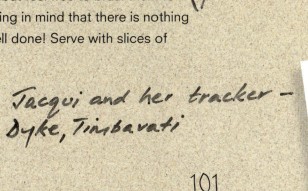

Jacqui looking for a wisdom tooth

Jacqui and her tracker – Dyke, Timbavati

Big Brother's Braai

My brother Steve, another good Eastern Cape boy, reminded me of this story about the farmers in the Bathurst district, near Port Alfred, who were upset with the state of disrepair of the public roads in the area. So they called a meeting with their local provincial administrative representative at their local – The Pig & Whistle, the oldest hotel in South Africa. The defensive local PA was vehemently denying there was anything wrong with the roads. A fed-up local told the gathering of how, while driving on the Grahamstown-Bathurst road he spotted a set of ears in the road. He said, 'I swerved to miss the pothole 'cause I thought there was a vundla (scrub hare) hiding in it. But swaer, it was a blaaaddy donkey!' They fixed the road.

Take 4 T-bones, about 250 g each. About 4 cm thick per person is perfect.

Marinate them (preferably overnight, but for at least 1 hour) in a mix of 1 Tbsp olive oil, 1 Tbsp honey, 1 tsp cumin seeds, 1 tsp soy sauce, and the juice of 1 lime or lemon.

Grill over coals. (How you do it is up to you. I prefer about 5 minutes per side, turned once only, on coals that are just going grey, and then set aside for about 5 minutes so they are medium-rare. But braai tastes are so personal I would NEVER dictate.) Baste with the remaining marinade as you turn.

Jacqui always needs to be catered for. I always try to look for not only a great accompaniment but also a stand-alone meal for the more considerate, compassionate f***ing non-meat eaters …

Thinly slice 3 red onions and cook them in 1 tsp of olive oil over low heat for about 20 minutes, stirring occasionally. Add 1 tsp brown sugar and 1 Tbsp balsamic vinegar and cook for a further 10 minutes. Leave to cool.

Jacqui's hint: Get him to make LOADS of this. Refrigerate and use it as a relish, on salads, to zhoozsh up a pasta, as a topping on toasted breads, anything. It tastes stunning!

Meanwhile, slice 4 ripe tomatoes and lay them out on a platter. Drizzle with 2 Tbsp extra virgin olive oil. Spoon the cooled onions on top and sprinkle with toasted pine nuts, sesame seeds and pumpkin seeds. Crumble 100 g of mild goat's cheese over the salad and chop a few leaves of basil to scatter over the top.

CAFÉ 96
HOI AN COOKING CLASSES (6pm to 8pm)
& & & 🍴 & & &

DETAILS: A Hoi An cooking classes is an interesting and fun way to learn about the local cuisine. The demonstration takes about 1 hour- each person helps prepare the dishes and then sit down to enjoy the meal.

The Class is persented by Mr BUP- the café owner. He introduces you to the local ingredient, takes you through the preparation, and explains the HOI AN style of cooking.

Cooking classes can be booked for either lunch or dinner. Please ask inside or telephone 0510-910441.
Vina : 0914082390. To check on cooking class time.

LOCATION:
CAFÉ 96
96 Bach Dang Street
Tel : 0510-910441
Vina : 0914082390
Email : MTHV2000@yahoo.com

MENU :
* **FRIED WONTON** : Wheat flour steamed to produce a wrapping f shimp and pork. Wonton are fried in hot oil and garnished with market and crushed black pepper.

GRILLED FISH IN BANANA LEAF : Local ocean fish stuffed v lemongrass, corriander, onions sugar rhum …Fish is wrapped in banar barbequed for approximately 30 minutes.

VEGETABLE SPRING ROLLS : Market vegetables wapped with paper and pan-fried-Steamed.

SQUID SALAD : Thinly sliced squid sauteed and combined with , Vietnamese mint, lemon juice …

Our food contains no MSG and English Recipes.

Price : Prices are inclusive of cooking demonstration and meal. A mi persons is required.
US$ 5/ VND * 78,000 Per Person.
A VND 50,000 deposit, per person, is required at the time of bookin

*Please Note : Fried wanton are secret Recipes made by only 1 An. They are included in the meal, but are not part of the cooking

Something else …Ask Inside please !

96 Bach Dang Street   tel: 0510. 910441

Furthest point from the peak display is … Pretoria! ENE 61.2° / 15844 km from Banff Canada

Rough notes taken at a cooking class in Hoi An

BANFF GONDOLA
www.banffgondola.com
Box 1258, Banff, Alberta T1L 1B2

Ticket #: 2474024
Ticket printed on: Jan 03, 2007 13:59
Admit 1 ADULT
Price: $24.95

HÓA ĐƠN (GTGT)
BILL
Liên 2 (Khách)

Mẫu : 2
Ký hiệu : AA/2003
Quyển số : 1243
Số : 062118
Số thứ tự : ST-24297

VIETNAM
VƯỜN THƯỢNG UYỂN

Ngày 25 tháng 10 năm 2003
Time: 14:31:34
(Number) Ca SANG 25/10/2003

Đơn vị bán hàng: KHÁCH SẠN BẾN THÀNH Địa chỉ: 141 Nguyễn Huệ, Quận 1, TP. HCM
Điện thoại: (84-8) 829 2185 or (84-8) 829 3115 Mã số thuế: 03 00625210-002-1
Cơ quan: Đoàn/Phòng: (1US= 15,589 VND)
Họ tên khách:
Bàn số: 55 Số người: 1
Hình thức thanh toán: TM Mã số thuế khách hàng:

STT No.	DIỄN GIẢI Description	ĐVT Unit	SỐ LG Quantity	ĐƠN GIÁ Unit price	THÀNH TIỀN Amount
1	U060Y COFFEE	LY	1	18,000	18,000
2	U464D BEER TIGER DRAGHT	LY	2	27,000	54,000

The hotel where American Defence Forces held press conferences during the war in Viet Nam. These became known as the 5 o'clock follies! as they contained so much mis-information

Cộng (Sub total): 72,000
Tỉ lệ phí PV (Service charge rate): 5% Phí PV (Service charge):
Thuế suất GTGT (VAT rate): 10% Thuế GTGT (VAT amount): 7,560
Tổng Cộng (Total): 83,160

* TỔNG CỘNG : 83,160 VND (#5.33 USD)
** Số tiền viết bằng chữ: TÁM MƯƠI BA NGÀN MỘT TRĂM SÁU MƯƠI ĐỒNG CHẴN.

Khách Hàng
Guest's Signature

Thâu Ngân
Cashier

Phát hành theo công văn số 3461/TCT/AC ngày 09 tháng 10 năm 1998 của Tổng Cục Thuế.

YamaGoya Sushi
741 7th Ave
Fernie, BC V0B 1M0
GST# 131794687

Table #21
Trans#: 27529   Serv: Rich
1/8/07 8:45:52 PM   # Cust:2

                            Cost
1 Pop $1.50
1 Gyoza $5.25
1 Miso soup $3.00
1 Ahi Poke $6.25
1 Bowl of rice $2.00
1 Unagi roll $5.75
1 Sunomono salad $4.25
1 Snapper Sashimi $7.50
1 Kryptonite Roll $5.50
2 Organic Lager $9.50

              Net Total: $50.50
                    GST: $3.03
                    LST: $0.95

              TOTAL : $54.48
Thanks for dining at
      YamaGoya

But wait,

there's more!

Zhoozsh Scrambled Eggs

I usually manage to zhoozsh up everything I do … even my marriage proposal was extraordinary. I proposed to Jacqui in a deep pool on the brink of Victoria Falls with only a sliver of rock to protect us from being swept over the edge. Yellow-billed kites were wheeling overhead, ellies drinking in the river upstream, I could see hippos snorting water into the air and the sky was filled with rainbows. The day before we'd both had waterlogged and oxygen-deprived experiences while whitewater rafting. I'm sure the near-death encounter had something to do with my surprise proposal and Jacqui's surprising yes. We married at sunset on Buffalo Charge Rocks in the Kruger National Park – God's own church. Jacqui wore a dress she'd bought when we backpacked in central Vietnam, and her Hi-Tec hiking boots. Her loud, raucous, intoxicated gal pals completely took over. Yeah, yeah chicks rule. My mates were real girl's blouses. Their handbrake dates controlling their 'natural exuberance'. Transferring back to Jock Lodge you could hear Jacqui's friends shrieking and whooping for kilometres. Really. It was a memorable wedding for Reverend Gibbon Bogatsu too. On his trip back he and his wife, Dudu, got seriously revved by a very large bull elephant (probably infuriated by the Landrover of noisy females that had just passed him). The Rev said afterwards he thought it was time to meet his Maker!

Beat together well in a microwavable container: 4 eggs, 100 ml low-fat milk, a pinch of salt, plenty of ground black pepper, 1 tsp baking powder (this fluffs up the eggs), and 2 Tbsp finely chopped chives.

Microwave, mixing the cooked outer eggs with the uncooked inner mixture every 20 seconds, until the consistency is to your liking. Leave to stand for 2 minutes. Serve.

This is how Jeremy zhoozshes it up when he 'serves' this simple dish: he spoons the cooked eggs into a ramekin or small Tupperware just big enough for a portion. He then toasts bread and cuts out the centre of the slice just a bit bigger than the diameter of the ramekin. He turns out the egg onto the toast cutout, adds a dollop of chutney, HP, tomato or sweet chilli sauce and then garnishes it with fresh coriander and the tomatoes (see hint). And yes, the serve-it-in-bed option is a surefire winner, especially if the chef wants his eggs to be well done!

Jacqui's hint: A great accompaniment to this is also simple. Microwave 20 ml balsamic vinegar in a cup until reduced by half. Halve 6 mini plum tomatoes and put them in the cup. Spin them for a minute. Place a few tomatoes on one side of the eggs and drizzle a little reduced balsamic vinegar over.

Buffalo Charge Rocks, KNP, 3.5.03

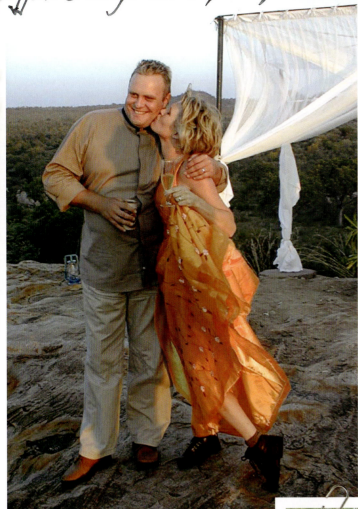

CONCENTRATE!

The noisy bunch

Me, Jacqui & David O'Sullivan, Fr. Gibbon Bogatsu and Dudu, with my mates Drysie and Doug with partners. Leaving Jock Lodge for the wedding

Proposal Pool, Vic Falls, Zambia '02. Just proposed — holding on to Jacqui — she wanted to jump over the falls!

L.A. gal on skates!

Potato Bake

Neither of us are gym bunnies but we both believe thinking regularly about going to gym does have a positive effect on one's physique. Jacqui exercises a little: flying off the handle, jumping to conclusions and roller-skating. This is one of her favourite carbo-loading meals. I think you only need to skate for about 69 km to work off this meal.

Boil about 10 medium to large potatoes in their jackets. Leave them to cool before removing the skins. Arrange a layer of thin slices of potato on the base of a baking dish. Salt and pepper ...

In a pan, fry: 300 g sliced mushrooms, 1 diced green pepper, 1 chopped onion, salt, black pepper, garlic and mixed herbs.

Using half the quantity, spoon an even layer of mushroom mixture over the layer of potatoes.

Spoon a layer of well-beaten cream over the mushrooms (I use the back of a spoon to spread it evenly and not too generously).

Spread an even layer of grated cheese.

Repeat: layer of potatoes, seasoning, mushroom/onion/green pepper, cream ... and finally cheese on top. Bake at 180 °C until golden brown (and it smells good!).

OK, you cut like....

NOOOO!.....

THIS.

Doug's Buttered Mealie

My pal Doug McCallum (who thinks bringing something to a party means supplying a few more litres of cane and coke) is a fisherman, a cook and a dopper of note. He first cooked these for us at Gavin Johnson's fishing camp, Mutemwa, in Zambia. Gavin (the fullback in the 1995 World Cup Springbok squad) is a modest and excellent guy. We baffled the lodge staff by insisting on moving the entire drinking session to a sandbank in the Zambezi. You could see them shaking their heads at the mad mazungus who left a perfectly good weatherproof lodge to sit in a river filled with smiling crocs, aggressive hippos, and under a sudden violent downpour and the very real threat of being struck by lightning. Eish!

Microwave 250 g butter in a flat dish. Grind 2 tsp black pepper into it. Because Doug has been a bachelor most of his life, preparing food has to be as quick and easy as his dates were. (I said WERE. For the record, that has all changed now that he's met his wife-to-be, Bok.) He buys the quick and easy, ready-made Chilli, Garlic & Ginger from Pick 'n Pay's Food Hall range. *Gooi* that in the butter and pepper mix. Roll the mealies in that sauce and braai. Keep basting them and don't let them go black.

Over-dopped in the Zambezi. New Years Day '04. Mutemwa, W. Zambia

I am very proud of the pictures I have of my wife buttering my mielie!

Osiyeza - the Crossing @ Mapai

Open Toasty

We like to go on our own self-drive southern African safari and load up our 4x4 and head out whichever way. Jeremy is the caterer and damn, he's good! He makes the best eat-on-the-go sarmies. One adventure took us through the Sango/Chicualacuala border from Zimbabwe into Mozambique. We were warned to attempt crossing the Limpopo only at Mapai. Expecting a ford, dyke, rocks or even just a row of sticks, we were astounded to pull up on the riverbank and find … nothing! A group of little kids in ragged clothing arrived and, chattering and gesticulating, they indicated they would show us a safe crossing point. If we had got stuck we could have been there for weeks or if the river was in flood we would have faced a lengthy two-day detour all the way to Maputo or back through Zim and Beit Bridge. We thanked the kids with food and clothing. Jeremy's T-shirts could double up as a shelter and one kid in one of the remotest areas in Mozambique is wearing a sarong from a very exclusive Indian island resort.

Take 2 slices of toasted wholewheat bread. Spread a bit of mayonnaise and sweet chilli sauce on each. Slice a generous amount of cold roast chicken onto them and top that with sliced avo. Salt and pepper to taste, then zhoozsh it up with some fresh, shredded rocket and coriander. A perfect meal for kids.

Jacqui – Bird watcher for all seasons – winter and summer!

Patch's Pan, Luvhuvhu Concession.

Outside Amber Suite, Sabi Sabi

Normandy Backpacking Egg Munch

I travelled to Normandy for the 60th Anniversary of the D-Day landings. It was a major occasion made poignant because it was probably the last time many of the veterans would be attending. I was deeply touched by the elderly, white-haired WWII soldiers who shared their war-time memories with me, and by watching these same elderly gentlemen talk with hard-bodied men with even harder eyes from the same regiment. It was a humbling experience and motivated me to write my book recounting the experiences of our own soldiers. Initially I stayed in Bayeaux, a quaint inland town liberated by British troops, but accommodation was scarce and I also backpacked through the region. An American camper shared this easy recipe with me.

Take one sturdy Ziploc bag per person. Crack 2 eggs into it, throw in bits and pieces of whatever you like: cheese, salami, and onion. Throw the bag into a pot of boiling water and leave for 2–3 minutes (depends on how much else you threw in). When the egg has 'set', remove and eat. It looks like an egg tortilla and there's no washing up!

Jacqui surrounded by interested men! Pre-parade in Bayeaux, Normandy, France, 2004

Very best friends

Gabriella + Jacqui parasailing

My big little girl

Gabriella's Get-out-of-Trouble Snack

Dan Moyane and I were neighbours for many years. Our daughters, Gabriella and Sina, grew up together and I'll never forget when the girls were about three years old my daughter was asked if she knew the difference between her and Sina. (Moronic question from an idiot.) She cocked her head, looked at the person and said, 'Yes, I'm taller.' Often Gabriella will help to cook but, being a teen, real life sometimes interferes with her social life. When she has to contribute to the preparation of a meal she will whip up this tasty yet ridiculously easy predinner snack …

Take a tub of plain low-fat cream cheese, upend on a plate, drizzle with sweet chilli sauce, chop up a few leaves of rocket and serve with Provita or crudités.

Veron's Scones

My mom used to make these for tuck. I don't know if I had cheese scones on this particular day, but it was a day that began like any other ... chemistry class ... squirting water up girls' dresses. Mr Ashmole sent me to the headmaster's office. Four jacks later I returned to wait outside the lab. Aha! Mr Ashmole's jacket. I smeared Vaseline in the pocket. It was a good idea at the time. Unfortunately, he returned before the end of class to get a pen from his pocket. Off to Headmaster Todd again, this time for six jacks. What a tough day. I needed a smoke. Unfortunately (again) I was bust by Mrs Paine and off I went to receive another six jacks. My grand total for the day was sixteen. Yet another record in my list of achievements and one that still stands.

Mix together: 1½ cups grated cheese, 1 cup plain flour, 1 level Tbsp baking powder, ½ tsp mustard powder, and 1 egg and enough milk to make up 1 cup.

Fill greased muffin pans to three-quarters full.
Bake at 220 °C for 10 minutes.

Flashing that bum from day one!

Oatlands Prep, Grahamstown

Our gorgeous big boy

The Bread that Rocky Ate

We had a dinner party for a dozen friends and had prepared Jeremy's sister Annie's nutty wheat bread – a meal on its own. However, when it came time to eat we couldn't find it. It wasn't in the oven and wasn't on the outside grill. It had vanished. Only the empty platter remained. Rocky! Only he is big enough to put his plate-sized paws on the counter and reach the bread. Close investigation of his whiskered mouth as he snoozed (maagie vol, oogies toe) did indeed reveal remnants of the loaf!

Rocky was badly abused and starved before being rescued by the SPCA and homed with us. He has major food issues so you can imagine how tricky the introduction of Patch, the cat, was. Rocky believes if it stands still long enough it's edible, and if it moves it's even more edible. Eat everything. He can eat his bowl of dog food in four seconds flat. Patch was a perfect snack-sized morsel. He would follow her around drooling, his nose touching the tip of her upright tail. She was completely unperturbed by this enormous dog that smacked his lips at her, smiled with his teeth and grunted with frustration. But he knows – you don't eat family.

You'll need: 4 cups of Nutty Wheat flour, 4 Tbsp brown sugar, 1 tsp salt, 1 tsp bicarbonate of soda, and 500 ml buttermilk.

Mix the dry ingredients together, and then add the buttermilk. Place the dough in a greased container and bake at 180 °C for 1 hour.

"Do you want to know how I made this bread?... ...oh. Perhaps not."

Canine Cuisine

Alex, our smallest and brightest dog, is a fussy eater, and a Christian. He'll eat dog food (shudder) if there truly is nothing else to eat and even that must be zhoozshed up with a sprinkle of minced garlic or, at the very least, a tablespoon of pure olive oil. Even cat food is better than what he is supposed to eat. We've always thought of him as a kinda cordon bleu canine … veeery particular. His only aversion is carrots. If he finds them in his food (another shudder) he carefully picks them out and places them around his bowl, where he graciously allows Rocky to polish them off once he has finished dining. Alex loves the park. No, that's an understatement, Alex LIVES for the park. Nothing on earth makes him happier than going to the park. While we were away my father house-, dog- and Patch-sat. But Alex, obviously feeling lonely without us, his ball-throwers, took himself off to the park on this particular Sunday morning. My dad searched the entire park grounds, but couldn't find him. Just then a church group emerged from the hall, and there among the congregation was Alex. He'd enjoyed church so much that he spent the entire morning there!

Throw 2 chicken carcasses, 250 g of chicken livers and 250 g of either gizzards or necks into a huge pot along with any vegetable offcuts (this is a great way of using the bits and pieces you would normally throw away). If you don't have any, then throw in a few carrots and potatoes. I also add about 300 g of bone meal (ask your butcher). Add 1.5 litres of water and a cube of vegetable or chicken stock and boil away for 2 hours. If necessary, add a bit of maize meal 15 minutes from the end to thicken. Vrrrrrr it all up with a hand blender (to the consistency your dog prefers) and pour it into containers.

On the beach with Alex & Jessie

Nog 'n Ding

If you use fresh ginger root and have any leftovers, peel the pieces and pop them in a glass jar. Top up with port. Refrigerate and serve the port ginger with cheese and water biscuits or cream crackers. And port, of course!

Alex in his beloved park!

Desserts...

Pavlova

Shannon, my sister, is one of those remarkable women who manages to look fantastic all the time, makes everything seem so effortless, never ages, is always gracious, keeps a beautiful home, has gorgeous well-mannered, bright children, and always looks terrific when her husband comes home to a cooked meal. I have no idea how she does it. She must have divine help from above (and Woolies and Spar). One warm summer evening after dinner, we were all sitting outside and she popped indoors to 'quickly make dessert'. A few minutes later she placed this heavenly dessert on the table. I was dumbstruck. How the hell did she do it so quickly? Fortunately we are related by blood and she had to tell me …

Whip 350 ml cream (add sugar only if you HAVE to have super sweet cream. I never add sugar believing that then entitles me to at least two more guilt-free helpings). Wash and chop up 1 peach, 1 nectarine, 1 banana, 1 kiwi fruit, and ½ a small pawpaw (actually, any soft fruit you enjoy). Spoon the cream into 1 large meringue nest about the size of a large soup plate. Top with the fresh fruit, 1 small tin mandarin orange segments, a handful each of blueberries and sliced strawberries, and then pour 1 small tin granadilla pulp over the top and serve. Prepare this just before serving otherwise the meringue goes soft. Place a sprig of mint on the top and tah-dah!

'Deeeeeelish!'

Gina

Christy + Shannon

Jacqui's tip: If you must go with extra sweet, sprinkle the strawberries with a packet or two of sweetener; it makes a world of difference.

Butterscotch Sherry Cake

Wilderness Safari's Savuti camp in northern Botswana has one of the most adrenaline-pumping game-viewing spots on earth (and great desserts!). The infamous Log Pile is a jumble of dead trees right next to a watering hole. You crawl into this rough circle of logs in the afternoon and wait until the elephants come down to drink. When they do you are completely surrounded as dusty, thirsty ellies jostle down to the water's edge. Seeing an elephant from this perspective is veeery different than from a vehicle or from far off on foot. You can count the eyelashes or examine the toenails! It is an experience that inspires awe and gratitude for their gentleness (yup, and fear).

Using a food processor, coarsely chop 100 g hazelnuts or pecan nuts. Sprinkle them over the base of a well-greased and floured tube (ring) baking pan.

Place 1 packet vanilla cake mix and 1 packet butterscotch instant pudding in the processor and pulse 2–3 times to combine.

Mix 130 ml water, 125 ml oil and 125 ml sherry with 4 beaten eggs and add to the cake and pudding mix, along with 3 ml ground cinnamon and a pinch of nutmeg. Process for 10 seconds. Scrape the mixture from the sides of the bowl and process for a further 25–30 seconds.

Pour the mixture into the prepared pan and bake at 180 °C for 40 minutes until a skewer comes out clean. Turn out onto a wire rack and immediately spoon the hot glaze over the top so that it soaks into the cake.

For the glaze, melt 90 g butter, and then add 150 g sugar and 45 ml water. Heat until the sugar has completely dissolved, stirring constantly. Add 90 ml sherry and bring to the boil. Remove from the heat and pour over the baked cake.

The Log Pile.

Savuti Camp, Bots.

Ellies in camp.
Duma Tau, Botswana

Mokoro, Xigera, Okavango

Patch — using Alex as cover to catch dragonflies

Baked Cheesecake

There are three things Jacqui loves ... chocolate, cheesecake and her cat, Patch. Jacqui went to interview a woman at the local SPCA. To cut a long story short she came home with three dogs and a cat. I'm highly allergic to cats. Highly. Jacqui phoned me to say there was this little grey cat, a cruelty confiscation, that just had to come home with her and could I get over my allergy? I knew it was a no-brainer. The cat or me? I'd be the one looking for somewhere to stay. This short-legged, sway-backed, stumpy-tailed, out of proportion, one-eyed cat arrived home. I wanted to call her Cyclops, but both the cat and Jacqui looked at me as if I was stale catnip. So Patch it was. She was permanently attached to Jacqui – even while she worked on her book, Patch would drape herself around Jacqui's neck. Not fun when furry fatty reached 5 kg. My eyes were red, swollen and so scratchy I could have clawed them out. I couldn't go near my wife for sneezing fits. And I sounded like I had flu. My voice is my livelihood so you can imagine how wonderful things were. It took three very long weeks before I could breathe and sound normal. Okay, I admit it, I'm cured. Okay?

Take 1½ packets of Tennis biscuits, crush them and mix with sufficient melted butter (not margarine!) until you have the right consistency for a crumb base. Press into a greased rectangular or round cake tin (I use a Pyrex dish, 30 x 18 cm and about 4 cm deep), keeping some aside for the topping.

Beat 1 large tin Ideal milk (kept in fridge overnight) until doubled in volume, add 500 g cream cheese, 2 eggs, 2 Tbsp flour, 1 Tbsp custard powder, and about ½ cup sugar (up to your taste buds as to how sweet you like it). Pour over crumb base.

Bake at 180 °C for about 20 minutes. Check by inserting a knife. If it comes out clean, the cake is ready. Sprinkle biscuit crumbs on top and toast under the grill for a nanosecond.

Patch, Jacqui's assistant. Editing Jacqui's book – An Unpopular War

Mama Sideropoulos' Sokolatina

Harry Sideropoulos is a man in love with food. He has an ongoing love-love relationship with food. It's his Greek heritage he claims. Even years after leaving my show, we still get together to meet, eat, drink and well ... eat some more. Often Harry will come over to our place with one of his mom Vivi's chocolate cakes – a super-rich creation guaranteed to put gazillions of kilos on between the lips and the hips. Seeing as Harry is part of the book, I feel I should share this story about him: We'd done a listener weekend in the bush and were flying back from the Sabi Sands. It was a little rural airport just outside Skukuza. The luggage was piled on trolleys in the same garden where the passengers waited. It was just after 9/11. Harry's bag started to buzz and vibrate. Porters leaped backwards and airline staff nervously approached the bag, ID'd the owner and asked Harry to open it after placing it a safe distance away. Of course we all crowded around and watched as Harry sheepishly pulled out his electric toothbrush! We never let him forget that. This serves 10 people, but only 6 Greeks or 4 chocoholics.

You'll need: 4 x 200 g Albany dark chocolate slabs, 2 x tins condensed milk, 5 x packets original boudoir finger biscuits, 250 ml full-cream milk, and 4 x 250 ml fresh cream.

Take the slabs of chocolate, break them into squares and place in a medium-sized pot (keep a few squares aside to grate over the surface of the cream at the end). Pour the condensed milk over the chocolate and place in a double boiler (*bain-marie*) on a very low heat, stirring occasionally. Grate two biscuits into a 40 x 25 cm Pyrex dish, covering its entire surface. (These crumbs act as lining and help prevent the cake from sticking to the dish.)

Pour the milk into a bowl. Take the biscuits and dip them one by one into the milk, then place them in the Pyrex dish next to each other. Crosshatch the layers by placing them one way then another way on the following layer. This ensures that the biscuit layers lock into each other, which makes it easier to cut once you are ready to serve the cake.

Once you have completed the first layer, spread the melted chocolate over the biscuits using a spatula, making sure that you haven't left any uncovered. Repeat with the second layer of biscuits, making sure that you place the biscuits in the opposite direction. Pour the remainder of the chocolate over the biscuits and spread evenly.

Pour the cream into a bowl and whip until stiff. Cover the entire surface of the chocolate-drenched biscuits with the cream ... and finally take the reserved blocks of chocolate and grate them over the top, finishing off the cake. Refrigerate for 4 hours.

Harry, Jacqui and me. Hard-a-party at Harry's 30th

'Talfred Tupperware Tart

Life is easy going in this attractive and bucolic backwater. The pace of life is as sluggish as the gentle Kowie River that flows through the Eastern Cape's Port Alfred. I knew Jeremy had hundreds of relatives down here, many of whom never moved far away from their family farms, which their ancestors ploughed out of virgin bush when they arrived in 1820. Who would've guessed Jeremy's bloodline was of Settler stock. Just don't mention the family skeleton – an unmarried woman who arrived on one of the first ships heavy with child! It still ruffles their feathers. Many of his family are pineapple farmers and Jeremy said I had to know the difference between a Swazi (cringe!) pine and a good Eastern Cape pine. If I couldn't, his uncles would make mincemeat of me. Eventually I was deemed knowledgeable enough to meet the clan. Whenever Jeremy tells an Eastern Cape joke his accent is very specific, with the slow drawl common to that area. I'd only heard the accent in the context of his jokes, so when I met all these people from 'Talfred (no resident calls it Port Alfred) and they all talked luhke theeeet swaer, jong, it took me awhiiiiiiile to reeeeeealize they were not having me on, but reeeeeally spoke that way!

This is an amazingly easy dessert. You'll need one of those plastic Tupperware shakers. A cap means to the top of the shaker lid, full to the brim. A seal refers to just the lid of the cap section.

Shake together: 1 cap milk, 1 cap flour, 1 cap sugar, 1 egg, 1 pinch salt, 1 seal of oil. Add 2 tsp baking powder. Spray an ovenproof dish with non-stick cooking spray. Line with 1 x 410 g tin of sliced apples.

Here you can sprinkle cinnamon (I have a heavy hand with this exotic spice) and add a handful of raisins or sultanas (not my favourite) if you like.

Pour the mixture over the apples. Bake at 180 °C for 30 minutes. Remove from the oven, pour over the syrup and cut into squares while still hot.

Make the syrup by melting 4 Tbsp butter and 4 Tbsp syrup together and pour over while both tart and syrup are hot. Serve with custard or ice cream.

On the Clumber farm outside Bathurst

Gabi + me, Mom + Dad + Sister Anne (mine) and Jacqui (also mine!) About 1/78th of my family is present here!

Fail-Safe, Kitchenless Camping Bananas

Only Jacqui would think this meal was fine for dinner when we camped in the dragon's back mountains of Chimanimani in eastern Zimbabwe. To get to the stonewalled mountain hut we took a near vertical route called Bailey's Folly. We started off okay but it soon started to rain. I was hiking in strops with a 20 kg backpack. Bad idea and my sweet wife was very quick to tell me so. 'You've got to have the right footwear,' she smugly stated before nipping up the mountainside another few hundred feet. Through clenched teeth I told her my shoes were FINE. It took me forever to reach the remote hut. Once there I did blame my strops and the weather, not my debatable level of fitness. I'm no damn racing snake! My irritating little partner said, 'There's no such thing as bad weather, only inappropriate clothing.' I wanted to push her off the mountain. The full moon, mountain peaks and towering cloud formations put on a show that night that made the climb worth every slippery step. It was the perfect place to spend Christmas. Four days later when we descended we heard the shocking news about the tsunami.

Taking your super-duper MacGyver tool, slit the banana lengthways (not all the way through) and gently press chocolate squares into the banana so that the squares stand upright. I have found the perfect ratio is 4 squares chocolate to 1 medium banana, but feel free to experiment. Wrap them in tinfoil and place them on the grill over the glowing coals of your campfire. If you don't have tinfoil, place them in a cooler part of the embers and watch carefully. The skin will blacken but that's fine. Pull them out the minute the banana is warm and squishy and the chocolate soft but still retaining its shape.

Morning coffee, Chimanimani

Zhoozsh Basics You Gotta Have

WET INGREDIENTS
Fish sauce
Sweet chilli sauce
Chutney
Tomato sauce
Soy sauce
Balsamic vinegar
White wine vinegar
Rice wine vinegar
Green fig preserve
Ginger
Garlic
Chillies
Lemon grass
Lemon juice
Olive oil
Sunflower oil

DRY INGREDIENTS
Salt
Pepper
Paprika
Garam masala
Turmeric
Ground cumin
Ground coriander or coriander seeds
Egg noodles
2-minute noodles
Couscous
Tastic rice with brown lentils
Wild and brown rice
Basmati rice

TINNED INGREDIENTS
Chopped tomatoes
Lentils
Butter beans
Chickpeas
Coconut milk
Bean sprouts

Conversion Tables & Oven Temperatures

METRIC	US CUPS	IMPERIAL	CELSIUS (°C)	FAHRENHEIT (°F)	GAS MARK
5 ml	1 tsp	3/16 fl oz	100 °C	200 °F	¼
15 ml	1 Tbsp	½ fl oz	110 °C	225 °F	¼
60 ml	4 Tbsp (¼ cup)	2 fl oz	120 °C	250 °F	½
80 ml	⅓ cup	2¾ fl oz	140 °C	275 °F	1
125 ml	½ cup	4½ fl oz	150 °C	300 °F	2
160 ml	⅔ cup	5½ fl oz	160 °C	325 °F	3
200 ml	¾ cup or ⅘ cup	7 fl oz	180 °C	350 °F	4
250 ml	1 cup	9 fl oz	190 °C	375 °F	5
			200 °C	400 °F	6
100 g	-	3½ oz	220 °C	425 °F	7
250 g	-	9 oz	230 °C	450 °F	8
500 g	-	1 lb	240 °C	475 °F	9
750 g	-	1¾ lb			
1 kg	-	2¼ lb			

Index

B

Baked Goodies
  'Talfred Tupperware Tart 137
  Baked Cheesecake 133
  Butterscotch Sherry Cake 130
  The Bread that Rocky Ate 123
  Veron's Scones 120

Beef Dishes
  Ali's Oriental Beef Salad 14
  Beef 'n Hansa 98
  Big Brother's Braai 102
  Oxtail 94
  Sadza & Nyama 93
  Samp & Beans 90
  Shin, Tomato & Beans 89
  Steak Casserole 97

C

Canine Cuisine 124

Casseroles
  Beef 'n Hansa 98
  Oxtail 94
  Steak Casserole 97

Chicken Dishes
  Chicken à la Antoontjie 68
  Ginger Coco Chicken Soup 34
  Greek Salad Dressing Chicken 67
  Madiba's Chicken Curry 71
  Open Toasty 115

Curries
  Madiba's Chicken Curry 71
  Mansfield QC (Quick Curry) 75
  T(ha)ime-Saving Curry Paste 72
  Thai Curries 72

D

Desserts 126–139
  Baked Cheesecake 133
  Butterscotch Sherry Cake 130
  Fail-safe, Kitchenless Camping Bananas 138
  Mama Sideropoulos' Sokolatina 134
  Pavlova 128
  'Talfred Tupperware Tart 137

F

Fish & Seafood Dishes
  Aftershock Salmon 52
  Grandma's Fish Pie 55
  Hot & Sour Fish Soup 33
  Jungle's Salmon Salad 20
  Pamushana Bream 59
  Seafood Stir-fry 64
  Sey-unique fish 56
  Simple Salmon Fish Braai 63
  Smoked Salmon Quick Bites 23
  Summertime Pan-fried Kingklip 48
  Tuna with Creole Coconut Curry and Parsley Polenta 60
  Zanzibar Fish Dish 51

L

Lamb Dishes
  Lamb Pasta 86
  Leg of Lamb à la Grecque 85

Light Meals & Accompaniments 106–125
  Doug's Buttered Mealie 112
  Gabriella's Get-out-of-trouble Snack 119
  Normandy Backpacking Egg Munch 116
  Open Toasty 115
  Potato Bake 111
  Zhoozsh Scrambled Eggs 108

M

Mains 36–103
  Aftershock Salmon 52
  Beef 'n Hansa 98
  Big Brother's Braai 102
  Chicken à la Antoontjie 68
  Couscous & Spicy Stir-fried Veg 40
  Grandma's Fish Pie 55
  Greek Salad Dressing Chicken 67

Lake Louise's Mock Lasagne 47
Lamb Pasta 86
Leg of Lamb à la Grecque 85
Macaroni Cheese with Crispy
   Bacon 44–45
Madiba's Chicken Curry 71
Mansfield QC (Quick Curry) 75
Noodle, Tofu & Smellee Wee
   Crunchee 39
Ostrich & Polenta 101
Oxtail 94
Pamushana Bream 59
Pork à la Pom 78
Pork Belly 80
Sadza & Nyama 93
Samp & Beans 90
Seafood Stir-fry 64
Seared Tuna with Creole
   Coconut Curry and Parsley
   Polenta 60
Sey-unique fish 56
Shin, Tomato & Beans 89
Simple Salmon Fish Braai 63
Spaghetti à la Shani 43
Steak Casserole 97
Summertime Pan-fried
   Kingklip 48
Sweet & Sour Pork 82
Thai Curries 72
Zanzibar Fish Dish 51
  Mince Dishes
    Lake Louise's Mock Lasagne 47
    Mansfield QC (Quick Curry) 75
    Spaghetti à la Shani 43

O
Ostrich Dishes
   Ostrich & Polenta 101

P
Pasta Dishes
   Lake Louise's Mock Lasagne 47
   Lamb Pasta 86
   Macaroni Cheese with Crispy
     Bacon 44–45
   Spaghetti à la Shani 43
Pork Dishes
   Pork à la Pom 78
   Pork Belly 80
   Sweet & Sour Pork 82

S
Salads
   Ali's Oriental Beef Salad 14
   Creamy Caesar Salad 13
   Hot Three-bean Salad 16
   Jungle's Salmon Salad 20
   Lentil-Feta Salad 18
   Summer Salad 23
Soups
   Ginger Coco Chicken
     Soup 34
   Hot & Sour Fish Soup 33
   Pho (Vietnamese Noodle Soup)
     28–29
   Potato Soup 26
   Vegetable Soup 30
Starters 10–35
   Ali's Oriental Beef Salad 14

Creamy Caesar Salad 13
Ginger Coco Chicken
   Soup 34
Hot & Sour Fish Soup 33
Hot Three-bean Salad 16
Jungle's Salmon Salad 20
Lentil-Feta Salad 18
Pho (Vietnamese Noodle Soup)
   28–29
Potato Soup 26
Smoked Salmon Quick
   Bites 23
Summer Salad 23
Vegetable Soup 30
Steaks
   Big Brother's Braai 102

V
Vegetarian Dishes
   Couscous & Spicy Stir-fried
     Veg 40
   Doug's Buttered Mealie 112
   Gabriella's Get-out-of-trouble
     Snack 119
   Hot Three-bean Salad 16
   Lentil-Feta Salad 18
   Noodle, Tofu & Smellee
     Wee Crunchee 39
   Potato Bake 111
   Samp & Beans 90
   Summer Salad 23
   Vegetable Soup 30
   Zhoozsh Scrambled
     Eggs 108

Acknowledgements

Thank you to the following people who contributed to this book, willingly or unwillingly:

Janine Blanckensee	Doug McCallum
Freda Bradfield	Roberto Mela
Rose Chinery	Dan Moyane
Joy Clack	Ravi Naidoo
Ali Coleman	Sidney Nyoni
Jungle Cong	Helder Pereira
Samantha Cowen	Ann Pike
Kevin Crambe	Ann Pritchard
Justine Drake	Ryno
Mark Drysdale	Janet Scully
Linda de Villiers	Harry Sideropoulos
Beverley Dodd	Southern Sun prep teams: Sandton & Cape Sun
Bill Gallagher	Brian Spilkin
Anton le Grange	Greg and Terry Volkwyn
Deone Maasch	Natasha Wadvalla
Dimitri Macris	Chris Watson
Peter & Veronica Mansfield	Agnes Zenani
Reza Mansfield	

Our latest addition — Honey helps with editing

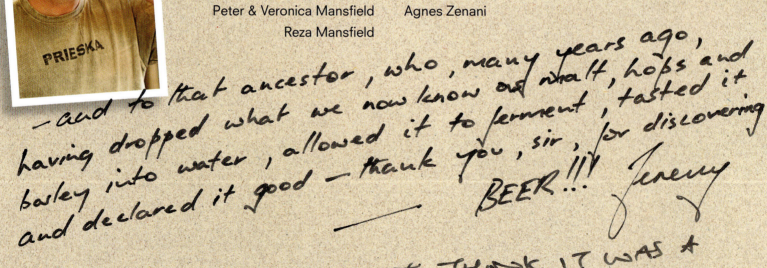

— and to that ancestor, who, many years ago, having dropped what we now know as malt, hops and barley into water, allowed it to ferment, tasted it and declared it good — thank you, sir, for discovering BEER!!! Jeremy

ACTUALLY LOVE, I THINK IT WAS A WOMAN. Jenny.